GW00506988

MALAWI OUR FUTURE OUR CHOICE

The selected essays of D.D. Phiri

D.D. PHIRI

Originally published in *The Nation* newspaper, Malawi

Selected and edited for this book by Judy Williams and John Williams

SOCIETY OF MALAWI (Historical and Scientific)
1946 - 2006
60th Anniversary

First published in Capetown in 2006 by
The Society of Malawi (Historical and Scientific)
PO Box 125 Blantyre Malawi
www.societyofmalawi.org

Printed by Hansa Print (Pty) Ltd Capetown

Bound by GraphiCraft (Pty) Ltd Capetown

Design by Petra Filip, www.wildvanilla.co.za, Capetown

ISBN 99908-36-02-7

ACKNOWLEDGEMENTS

John Williams, my husband, has throughout shared my enthusiasm for this publication, has helped select and edit the essays, and has provided support in innumerable ways.

My thanks go to D.D. Phiri for handing over to me, a virtual stranger, the only existing complete collection of his essays, contained within yellowing pages of *The Nation* newspaper; eight sacks of them, to be precise.

Thanks too to my visiting friend Elisabeth Kelvin-Davies with whom I spent many enjoyable evenings chatting and snipping our way through 12 years of newspapers.

For the painstaking task of typing the essays from the original newsprint, I am grateful to John and to Xanthe Lithgow who generously volunteered their time.

Sincere thanks go to all sponsors and subscribers who kindly provided advance funds to enable this book to be published.

Frank Johnston has been generous with his advice and his contacts.

The Nation newspaper has kindly supported the reproduction of the essays as originally published in its pages.

Many others have provided help for which I am most grateful.

In celebrating its 60 years of preserving and promoting the history and culture of Malawi, it is fitting that the Society of Malawi should publish the work of D.D. Phiri, one of Malawi's great modern writers and historians.

CONTENTS

INTRODUCTION

Freedom is hammered out on the anvil of discussion, dissent, and debate.
Hubert H Humphrey

During the colonial era civil servants who wished to write and publish books or articles were required to submit their work to their head of department or to the secretariat for approval before they could publish. This was a long, exasperating and traumatic process which dissuaded many officers from publishing – to their own and to society's loss. Then, apparently quite suddenly, at about the time of Independence in 1964, there seemed to be a remarkable change, for officers discovered that their papers were being treated promptly, sympathetically and helpfully. They discovered, too, that their submissions were being dealt with by officers newly appointed to the Administrative Service who had recently returned to their home country in response to the call to help Malawi with their education and experience. One of these officers was Desmond Phiri, who joined the Service in June 1964, three weeks before Independence Day. He was one of eight Malawian university graduates appointed in 1964 who joined the two Malawian graduates already in the Administration. The country owes a considerable debt to these graduates and the score of their colleagues trained internally at the Institute of Public Administration, who significantly added to the effectiveness of the civil service at a time when, with the departure of expatriate Administrative Officers, there was the distinct possibility that the service might collapse.

Desmond Dudwa Phiri was born on 23 February 1931. Both his parents were elders of the Free Church of Scotland and his father was a school teacher. He was educated first at local village schools and then at Loudon and Livingstonia before going to Blantyre Secondary School where in 1949 he obtained his Junior Certificate. He went to Zambia where he was employed in a bus company and three years later, in 1952, he moved to Dar es Salaam in Tanganyika where he was employed as an Accounts Clerk in the civil service, eventually becoming a Senior Commercial Officer in 1963 – by which time Tanganyika was already independent. Whilst in Dar es Salaam he continued his studies and passed two O level examinations, four A levels, and the London University B.Sc. (Economics). A little later he studied at the London School of Economics and Political Science and secured the Post-Graduate Diploma in Economic and Social Administration. On his return to Malawi he was appointed to the Ministry of Finance and then to the Diplomatic Service where he was Commercial Attaché and First Secretary at the Malawi Embassy in Bonn, Germany. He retired from the Service in 1976 with the rank of Under Secretary, and set up the distance learning institute – named the Aggrey Memorial School – which has provided effective and affordable educational courses to many Malawian students unable to study in any other way.

It is important to present this mini-biography, because many of the elements in it have influenced, and help account for, the content of the writing to which Desmond has devoted himself in the past decade and a half. And what are these elements? They include a great respect and thirst for knowledge and education, derived at least in part from his school teacher father and his family up-bringing. There is an emphasis on Economics and Politics which flows from the subjects that fired his imagination and which he studied for his degree and diploma and about which he has thought a great deal in his 'retirement', and they are often accompanied by an interest in the problems of poverty and of agriculture, crucially important matters in his home country. There are clear indications, too, of his love of Africa and particularly of Malawi.

Though these are the most obvious elements in his writing there are others which are less dominant but none the less important – philosophy, demography and literature, for example – and the various elements are sometimes combined, notably in the overlap of the fields of economics and politics, politics and society. The result is a wide range of subjects which he has mastered and which make up the content of his extensive writing. But this present collection of his essays is but a part of his literary output, for he has written an astonishing total of seventeen books. In his series *Malawians to Remember* he has written the biographies of Inkosi Gomani II, James Frederick Sangala, Charles Chinula, John Chilembwe and Dunduzu Chisiza. He is one of the co-authors of Dr Bakili Muluzi's *Democracy with a Price*. He has written, too, four novelettes in ChiTumbuka, and two important histories: *From Nguni to Ngoni*, a history of the Ngoni exodus from Natal and Swaziland to Malawi, and *History of Malawi: from the Earliest Times to 1915*. There seems no end to the range and volume of his literary output.

It is not simply the range and volume of his output, however, that is important, for the period in which it has been produced should not pass without special notice, spanning as it does all but the first year or so of the period of Dr Banda's Presidency and the First Republic – *The Chief's Bride* was published in 1968 – and the Second Republic, covering the two terms of Dr Bakili Muluzi's Presidency and the current Presidency of Dr Bingu wa Mutharika. That is both a very long period and one of great change especially politically, particularly with two of the Presidents being graduates in politics! The current collection of Desmond Phiri's essays begins in 1993, almost with a fanfare: 'Citizen, what about our next President?' Its publication marks – almost heralds in – the post-Dr Banda openness and freedom of expression, particularly in the public discussion of politics and society. In earlier post-colonial times it would have been profoundly imprudent to initiate public discussion of such sensitive matters as Malawi's poverty, debt and emigration. But from 1993 onwards, his essays in *The Nation* have ranged widely and appeared regularly, stimulating the readers to think about the issues he raises and discusses, to form an opinion on them and hopefully to do something about them. Hannah Arendt, the German-born American philosopher and political scientist, would have approved:

Opinions are formed in a process of open discussion and public debate, and where no opportunity for the forming of opinions exists, there may be moods – moods of the masses and moods of individuals, the latter no less fickle and unreliable than the former – but no opinion.

Society and the Government in Malawi have provided the opportunity for open discussion and public debate. Desmond Phiri seized, and continues to seize, that opportunity and thereby has bestowed a great blessing on his fellow countrymen and women. In January 2005 the Malawi *Sunday Times* invited its readers to nominate Malawians for inclusion on a list of the twenty greatest Malawians. Dr Banda came top of the list, John Chilembwe second, Dr Bakili Muluzi third, other great Malawians followed and, to his own astonishment, Desmond Dudwa Phiri came twelfth. Readers of this collection of essays will not share his surprise. Instead they will share the opinion of those *Sunday Times* readers who voted for him.

Colin Baker

<u>23 September 1993</u>

CITIZEN, WHAT ABOUT OUR NEXT PRESIDENT?

L ooming large in the minds of most Malawians is the question: who is to be our next president? I cannot answer this. What sort of president will he or she be? This too is difficult for me to predict. What qualities of leadership should our president have? On this I can venture an opinion.

In the late 1950s I read two books on rulers of men which have kept my eyes open ever since. In *Nationalism in Colonial Africa* by Thomas Hodgkin I was surprised but pleased to learn that the Senegalese poet, philosopher and playwright Leopold Sedar Senghor was intellectually superior to the average of the British and French Cabinet. Senghor, as you may know, later became the first President of his country and after two decades in office he voluntarily stepped down in favour of a younger man, Abdou Diouf.

In one of his autobiographical writings the best-selling British author W. Somerset Maugham stated that he had observed that it did not require superior intelligence to be a ruler, or words to that effect.

As if to confirm what I had heard, I saw Nigeria giving genuine executive power to the late Abubakar Tafawa Balewa, a school teacher of no intellectual distinctions, in preference to Dr Nnamdi Azikiwe (Zik), the father of Nigerian independence and a versatile genius.

India has produced great men in all fields of life, science, economics, philosophy, business, name it. Its first Prime Minister Jawaharlal Nehru was a great man of great intellectual accomplishments, a product of British public school education with qualifications in Law. Both Nehru's daughter Indira Gandhi and his grandson Rajiv Gandhi were college dropouts. After Nehru's death the people of India entrusted their country to them, and they performed quite well despite their tragic end.

To answer what sort of president should we have in Malawi we need to ask first what sort of country Malawi should be. No doubt we want to continue living in a land free of civil strife. The MCP puts great store on peace. But this is a minimum of what the country deserves. There is peace in a zoo, and some of its inmates seem to be well-fed. But if you think they are happy, go and open the gates and see if they will remain there.

In the Second Republic of Malawi, peace must exist side by side with freedom and justice. Our next president must be a respecter of human rights. Like the rest of the citizens, whatever he does must be within the law of the land. No one should be above the law.

He does not have to be a university graduate. If he is, so much the better, because managing a modern State requires a good deal of intellect. He must have education and intelligence enough to understand the problems of a modern State; most of these problems revolve around such macro-economic issues as unemployment, economic growth, inflation, distribution of wealth and balance of payments. He must be a person who spares time to read newspapers and books and understands current international problems. Above all, he must be a person who should know when to seek advice from technocrats around him. Modern problems are so intricate that no honest person can claim to understand them all.

Above all, our next president should be a Malawian first and a member of his tribe, religion, clan or what not last. He may be Moslem, Catholic, Protestant, Hindu, Bahai or animist. Once he is president, he should not allow these affiliations to have undue influence on his attitudes and policies in national affairs.

Once elected, a good president realises that he is there to serve all people, even those who did not vote for him, and even those who do not belong to his party. It is unfair for a ruler to demand taxes and allegiance from everyone, even members of the opposition, and yet confer titles and beneficence only on his party activists. To restrict appointments in statutory bodies and invitations to public functions only to members of his party is a sure way of turning political rivalry into animosity. Let us have something better than this.

The old multi-party democracies have something to teach us about handling one's political opponents. In the 1950s a brilliant lawyer in the United States called Adlai Stevenson twice stood for the Presidency against the more famous General Eisenhower. On both occasions he was defeated. At his second defeat General Eisenhower appointed him US representative to the United Nations. Last year after British elections it was widely speculated by newspapers that victorious John Major was going to appoint his defeated rival Neil Kinnock as UK representative to the EEC.

This is the kind of president Malawi now should have, someone who is charitable to all, and bears malice against none. President Dr Banda's style has been to denigrate and drive into hiding those who had dared to oppose him. In a multi-party Malawi we must learn to eat and drink with those whose political beliefs we do not share.

Even if a person is affiliated to a rival political party, if he has the best experience to chair meetings of a statutory body like Railways, Escom, Admarc, appoint him. It is one way of softening the blow of defeat. Multi-party democracy is about live and let live. The MCP policy was: die so that I may live; rot in jail or exile while I prosper.

The president-to-be should be a person of simpler tastes for the good things in life. He may repeat Ngwazi Banda's maxims that so long as the people of Malawi have enough food to eat, decent clothes, and houses that do not leak, it does not matter if they do not have other things. But he must not erect more palaces. Or seek to upgrade those we already have. The poor taxpayer of Malawi (even if he does not pay poll taxes, he pays sales taxes, customs duties on what he buys) must not be compelled to support high living while he himself dwells in shanties and hovels.

Mahatma Gandhi, who started his political career in South Africa, later wrote in his biography about Paul Kruger, President of the Transvaal, "President Kruger's house was very, very modest, unostentatious ... without a garden and not distinguishable from other houses in its neighbourhood..."

At that time, the end of the 19th century, the Transvaal was already fabulously rich, thanks to the gold mines of Johannesburg. Surely, if presidents of wealthy countries can live modestly, those of poorer countries can manage to do so as well.

Our next president should preferably be a married man with children. He might understand better the agony of those whose children or parents die or rot in jail. He might find it easier to reason: If I treat other people's children and *mbumba* inhumanely, won't someone who comes after me do the same to my children and *mbumba*.

A president must be a man with a clear mission to achieve for the country, not just for himself. He must not look at the State House or the presidential convoy as a goal in itself. Charles de Gaulle in his memoirs wrote, "All my life I have thought of France in a certain way... France is not really herself unless she is in the front rank. France cannot be France without greatness." De Gaulle became great not because he wanted to make himself great but because he set out to make France great. You sir, if you are aspiring for the presidency, what do you want to achieve for Malawi?

3

Malawi is facing gargantuan problems; economic, social, political. We need an energetic leader, highly committed to the welfare of his people. While we do not want another dictator, we must not swing to the opposite of placing on the throne a dormant man or a man of straw who will be despised by all and respected by none just because he cannot act fast and decisively. A president need not be a dictator, but he must certainly be a leader of his country, a captain of the ship of state.

He must be the type of leader who will seek advice but will not be afraid to act; and then accept responsibility for the outcome of his decisions. A person who arrogates all the kudos to himself when things go well, but blames his ministers or civil servants when his decisions turn sour is likely to punish the innocent. The right leader will be willing to go back to the polls if he thinks the country is behind him despite the clamour of the Opposition. Once it is clear that he is no longer fully supported by the majority of the country he will voluntarily step down. He will not deceive himself or others that the country cannot survive without him. A hundred years hence there will be people here without him. In the survival of a nation only God is indispensable.

My models of strong leaders are Charles de Gaulle of France, Jawaharlal Nehru of India, Margaret Thatcher, Julius Nyerere, Leopold Senghor, Ronald Reagan.

Let us hope that our next Constitution will make provision for a vice-president or prime minister. This is common practice in most countries. It is one method of ensuring smooth succession in case the incumbent president is incapable of undertaking his duties due to illness, absence from the country or something more serious.

Who should be candidates for the vice-presidency? The qualities of leadership expected of a vice-president are not materially different from those expected of a president. But for this portfolio first chance should be given to the ladies. And who are they? Edda Chitalo, Vera Chirwa, Rose Chibambo, Margaret Mlanga, on the reformist side. On the status quo side my preference would be Kate Kainja, Nellie Mseula, Lydda Maganga. And of course the Mama herself. She has a wealth of experience for the government to fall on. But not that lady by the River Songwe or that one by the River Lilongwe. The country cannot afford the politics of Jezebel.

31 August 1994

THE 'AFRICAN PERSONALITY' REVISITED

Soon after Ghana attained independence in 1957, its first president Dr Kwame Nkrumah convened a meeting of independent African states in Accra. There were only eight such states at that time.

In his address to the conference, Nkrumah said, *inter alia*, "We the delegates ... in promoting our foreign relations must endeavour to seek the friendship of all and the enmity of none... This will enable us to assert our own African personality, and to develop according to our own ways."

Dr Nkrumah was a very influential man. Soon after, African intellectuals all over were debating and expounding their own concepts of the African personality. A famous South African author, E. Mphahlele (his novel *Chirundu* has a Malawian background) discussed the concept in his book *African Image*. Dunduzu Chisiza Sr. referred to it as African outlook.

Hitherto, Africa south of the Sahara had been given an unfavourable image by people beyond the seas. They said Africa was a dark continent, its people had invented nothing, not even the wheel; that Africans had no history of their own until the advent of the slave trade and European colonial rule. Even great philanthropists who had spent their lifetime rendering yeoman service among Africans, like Dr Albert Schweitzer of Lambarene, Gabon, could only speak patronisingly of Africans as mere children who dwelt on the present, never thought of the future.

As one country after another attained independence, the world view of the African personality became brighter. During the Cold War days both the West and the Eastern bloc lionised African diplomats in their capitals, and courted their support at international conferences.

The Cold War is over. More than thirty years have passed since most African countries hoisted their own flags in place of the Union Jack and the French tricolour. Now what view does the world have of the African continent and its people? Not a very flattering one, I am afraid.

A feature writer in the American *Time* magazine of August 15, 1994, sees Africa as a "lost continent, a modern Atlantis," he also sees this continent of

500 million inhabitants south of the Sahara (excluding South Africa) as producing less goods than 10 million Belgians, and exporting less than Hong Kong with its 5 million people.

To most people beyond our continent, Africa is home to despots, sanguinary civil wars, land-scorching famines, and Aids. Surely, the African personality is anything but endearing.

Let us not close our eyes to the realities of Africa. We can no longer blame colonialists and racialists for our handicaps and lacklustre personality. By taking an accurate stock of our assets and liabilities, we might start afresh on a more hopeful road to development.

A *Time* magazine columnist gives the people of Africa, and those of Senegal in particular, credit for being free of religious intolerance. He notes that for two decades Senegal, a predominantly Moslem country, had a Christian president. Perhaps he has not heard of the election results in Malawi since he does not extend a similar compliment to us.

Another African asset is greater willingness to accommodate women's talents. Since colonial days there have been criticisms of the way men in Africa treat their women. One thing is certain: we Africans have no theory about gender inferiority or superiority. The relationship between men and women has been governed by social and economic circumstance.

From the day most Africans started exercising their right to vote, men and women have queued together. There have never been suffragettes in Africa, because men never stood in the way of women's political rights.

In Britain, after centuries of democratic reforms, it was only at the end of the First World War that women were accorded the right to vote, thanks to the untiring efforts of the suffragette, Mrs Pankhurst. On the continent of Europe, in one country it is only about five or ten years ago that women were allowed to vote.

During the 73 years that Britain ruled this country, I doubt if any of their women were appointed as District Commissioner, Judge or Director of a department. We have scored better on this.

But we have blatant shortcomings too. We Africans have acquired Western appetites for material wealth, but have not yet acquired the virtue of enterprise, inventiveness and thrift on which the wealth of Europe and North America have been founded.

Highly educated and trained Africans prefer to stay on in Europe or America rather than go back home because they say their own countries do not offer them salaries high enough to support the standards of living which they have got used to in those temperate lands. Yet these men were born in round thatched mud huts. As children they had gone about barefoot. If they won't come home to make the necessary sacrifices, who is to create the wealth of Africa? Are they waiting for someone to develop Africa and then invite them home to come and enjoy its affluence?

At the turn of the century, a young German was in America, working for the famous inventor, Thomas Alva Edison. Having gained enough experience, the young Deutschlander returned home, set up a firm of his own that became one of the engines of growth in his country and still bears his name: Siemens. If during the next 30 years or so Africa is to be a better continent than it is now, its sons and daughters both at home and abroad must take to heart what the late John F. Kennedy, as President of the USA, said to his people, "Ask not what your country can do for you – ask what you can do for your country." Today in Africa, as in the days of Cecil John Rhodes, there is so much to do, but very little has been done.

What can you do for your country? Search for a calling in which you have the aptitude and perhaps the talent. The greatness and prosperity of a country does not depend only on those who are in high places. Monuments have been erected to men and women in all walks of life, to those who held high positions in life, and to those who never did, but who rendered a service that benefited mankind.

The days of denouncing colonialism and racialism are gone in Africa. The challenge now is to produce the Henry Fords, the Thomas Edisons, the Siemens, the Shakespeares, the Isaac Newtons. It is such persons that will give a better image to the African continent. Despots have done the continent a lot of harm.

2 May 1995

DR AGGREY'S TEACHINGS AND MODERN TIMES

Few young people born during the post-African Independence era that one meets these days appear to know who Dr Aggrey was; fewer still know what he did and taught. This is a pity but it is understandable.

Up to about the mid-1950s no name in Africa south of the Sahara was as revered and loved as that of Dr Aggrey. It was when they heard of the emerging political giants like Dr Kwame Nkrumah of Ghana, Dr Nnamdi Azikiwe of Nigeria and Mzee Jomo Kenyatta of Kenya that ambitious young Africans now began to speak less and less of Dr Aggrey.

People become famous for either their deeds or their ideas. Aggrey was a great teacher. His former students, like Kwame Nkrumah at Achimota College, Ghana and in North Carolina, United States, spoke highly of him. But the rest of Africa recognised him as 'Aggrey of Africa' because of his philosophy and the ideas which helped many Africans to look at themselves and their race more positively.

Dr James Kwegyir Aggrey was born in the Gold Coast (Ghana), a member of the Fanti tribe, in 1875. At the turn of the century he went to the United States, North Carolina in particular, where after taking several degrees including a Doctorate in Divinity he settled down to teach.

In 1921 Dr Aggrey was appointed a member of the Phelps-Stokes Commission on African education. Not many people outside Ghana had heard the name Aggrey before, but from this year on his was to be a household name, adored in most places of learning. Wherever he went, he enthused the youth of Africa with ambitions for higher education and pride in their colour and culture which were despised in those days, not just by people of other races but by some of the Africans themselves.

On his visit to Nigeria in 1921, a 16-year-old boy was enthralled with Dr Aggrey's message. Later that boy, as the world famous Dr Azikiwe, was to write in his autobiography *My Odyssey,* "At Tinubu Methodist Church one day I listened to a sermon which saturated my whole being. I became spiritually electrified. It then dawned upon me that life had a meaning and I had a mission to fulfil. Dr Aggrey spoke about his life and he had come to announce that 'Nothing but the best is good enough for Africa'. He ended with words like these 'If I, one of you, could go to the New World and make a man of myself, then you can too. May God help you, Amen.'"

Aggrey gave young Azikiwe a book called *Negro Education: A study of the Private and Higher Schools for Coloured People in the United States*. Four or five years later Benjamin Nnamdi Azikiwe was one of the many young men who, inspired by Aggrey, went to the United States with little more than sea-passage money to seek the golden fleece of American education using the methods Aggrey himself had used: taking up any odd jobs so as to raise college tuition funds.

After his death in 1927 several biographies of his life appeared, the most comprehensive by Rev E.W. Smith. A slim sketch of his life also appeared in Chinyanga and was on sale in Claim Bookshops until the late 1970s.

In the pre-independence era history lessons in primary schools in Malawi and other English-speaking African countries included topics on eminent Africans. In this way we heard of John Tengo Jabavu of South Africa, King Moshoeshoe of Lesotho, Bishop Crowther of Nigeria, Apolo Kagwa of Uganda, and of course Dr Aggrey, whose achievements were by far the most inspiring.

Though some of the ideas he expounded are no longer revolutionary or enthralling, they can be adapted to match the Africa and the world of today.

Dr W.E.B. DuBois, a black American and moving spirit of the Pan African Congress, had written at the beginning of this century, in his book *The Souls of Black Folk*, that colour of skin would be a dominant problem of the 20th century.

As if to confirm this, wherever Dr Aggrey went in Africa, he found Africans evincing inferiority complexes because of their black skins. He told them that a person should be proud of the colour God had given him. If he himself died, and God wanted to send him back to earth he would ask to be sent back darker than he was.

Revolutionary blacks like followers of Marcus Aurelius Garvey and Aggrey's own student at Achimota, Kwame Nkrumah, thought that Africans' first concern was not cooperation with their masters but regaining their freedom.

Yet today, cooperation between people of different races, tribes and religions has become more urgent than ever. The world has shrunk so much that in every country people of different races, tribes and religions cannot help living in close proximity. If you do not believe in the sort of cooperation and coexistence that Aggrey advocated, just look at what has happened in Rwanda and Yugoslavia. The 'bloody' Boer of South Africa has become the beautiful Afrikaner by repudiating apartheid.

Wherever he went (he came to Malawi in 1924) Aggrey met young people complaining that their white rulers were denying them opportunities for advancement. He told them: "Make use of what you have to get what you want," advice that is still valid today but that is as unappreciated as ever. Aggrey was preaching self-help and self-reliance. These are the virtues which have transformed ordinary persons into geniuses or leaders in their chosen fields. You cannot achieve much in life if you wait for assistance from other people.

In the past, mention the name of Aggrey and you reminded someone about the parable of the eagle which had grown up among chickens. One morning a naturalist had taken it to the hills and reminded it that it was an eagle, that its place was up in the air, not on the ground, that it was destined for greater tasks.

Aggrey was telling Africans both as individuals and groups to aim higher. Today, as ever, you have not fulfilled all your duties if you have not rescued someone from despondency and encouraged him to make a success of his life.

Wherever Aggrey went in Africa, he found missionaries were teaching Africans to despise African culture. He told them "eliminate by substitution". These days we still come across people who advocate abolition of certain customs without suggesting something that should take the place and fulfil the virtues of the custom that is now condemned.

For example, if you abolish *lobola*, what system do you propose that will provide the family stability which the *lobola* custom provided. If you abolish polygamy, what do you do with a woman who cannot fend for herself. The Malawi Youth and the MYP have become stinkers, but what substitutes have we found to carry on the more positive functions of these bodies? The Youth used to assist the police in tracking petty criminals in townships. The Pioneers were engaged in productive work at training bases.

Wherever he went Dr Aggrey appealed for the education of women; said he, "Educate a man, you educate one person; educate a woman, you educate a family." No need to elaborate or adapt.

THE PATRIOTIC CITIZEN

T*he Concise Oxford Dictionary* defines a patriot as a person who is ready to support or defend his or her country.

With most people the word patriot conjures up the figure of soldier kings or princes like England's Alfred the Great or Scotland's Prince Edward, the Young Pretender. Crossing the English Channel, they recall the exploits and fate of the armed maid Jeanne d'Arc, who tried to drive out English invaders, or Charles de Gaulle, who stood up against the Nazi might, crying "France has lost a battle but not the war."

Here in Africa we attribute greatness and patriotism to those who led *satyagraha* or guerrilla wars against colonial rulers. Achievers in other walks of life, perhaps with the exception of sport, are hardly noticed.

Years ago in a Geneva bookshop I chatted with a Zairian who had just taken a doctorate degree from a Swiss or French university. His English was 'a little' and my French was 'un peu' but both of us spoke Swahili. I asked him if he was going to his country as a university don. *"Hapana nitakwenda Kusema siasa tu."* No, I am just going to talk politics.

Politics has been a great attraction to most educated Africans because it is the shortest route to the standard of living colonial Mandarins used to display here. Soon after winning independence, some people who had been mere clerks but had played prominent roles in liberation campaigns were given positions formerly held by Oxford graduates, and some were allocated houses in which they had once served as domestic servants.

A patriot of today should be a person who thinks and speaks along the lines recommended by Frank Buchman, founder of the religious movement called Moral Rearmament (MRA). At the end of the Second World War this movement used to hold regular meetings in Switzerland. Many educated Africans were given free tickets to attend the gatherings. They came back saying they had been impressed with the idea that in trying to solve problems we should think of *what* is right, not *who* is right. We no longer hear of the MRA, but I think some of its principles are still sound.

If we directed our thoughts more towards what is good for the country, and less on who ought to have the big job, political and social conflicts would be fewer. A patriotic citizen should be like the woman in Solomon's court who let the other woman have the baby rather than allow it to be wrenched in twain.

Losing an election in Africa is a traumatic experience. Some people will respect democratic institutions if they are the winners. Those that lose become very bitter towards the winner and wish for anything to happen that might force the winner off the political pedestal. Already here some papers are urging the MCP leaders to organise civil disobedience against the UDF/Aford government and to replace it by one of their liking.

The wishes of the millions of people who voted for the present government are to be shoved aside as happened in Haiti. The Constitution says general elections should be held every five years. But no, this is too far off for those who either lost themselves or saw their mentors lose.

After Jimmy Carter, former President of the United States, lost his second bid for the presidency, he toured several countries of Africa as he is still doing now. At a reception in Zimbabwe the host speaker made bitter attacks on the President of the USA and the USA itself. Carter walked out of the room. He could not applaud someone making derogatory and unfair criticism of either his country or his President even though that President had snatched victory from himself. He was putting the honour of his country above personal *schadenfreude*.

Here in Malawi, reading papers hostile to the Government reveals *schadenfreude* on a grand scale. The writers seem to be praying that government's efforts to resuscitate the economy (which had already declined while the MCP was in control) should come to naught. But if the efforts to reduce inflation, increase employment opportunities and strengthen the kwacha fail, are we not all going to suffer? Never mind, so long as this speeds the removal of the holders of the office I pine for.

In 1871, the country that had produced such great rulers and conquerors as Louis XIV and Napoleon was itself badly humiliated by the Prussians. A scientist by the name of Louis Pasteur (1822–95) decided to devote himself to the conquest of microbes that ruined the health of millions of human beings. He believed that his scientific achievements would benefit mankind and uphold the great name of France which had been damaged by military defeat. His people and the world treated him as a hero, just as in the 1960s Dr Jonas Salk of the USA, discoverer of a vaccine against polio was, according to the London *Economist* of 1 July 1995, ranked with Winston Churchill and Mahatma Gandhi in opinion polls.

Albert Einstein (1879–1955), born a German Jew but later a naturalised American, achieved fame as a mathematician and physicist. Whatever the Theory of Relativity may mean to some of us, his discoveries paved the way for atomic inventions. In America he spent a considerable amount of time campaigning against misuse of his atomic discoveries. But whatever influence he exerted in public affairs, it paled in comparison with his achievements in science, and he knew it. When the new State of Israel was founded in 1948 Einstein was invited to become its head of state. He declined the honour, saying that though he understood a bit about the laws of physics, he did not understand those of human nature. Patriotism sometimes must take the form of humility. Know your strengths and weaknesses and keep to your side.

When the American library was in Blantyre years ago, one of the books I borrowed, and read with avidity, was the biography of the great inventor Thomas Alva Edison. After all the years that I have passed, I still recall reading that one of his assistants in the laboratory was a young German called Siemens, and that this young man later returned to his country and founded the great firm that still bears his name. The vast opportunities to become rich in America did not make him forget his own country. Neither do they make patriotic Asians forget their roots.

The magazine *Business Week* of 3 July 1995 features on its cover two Indians in business suits. Inside the magazine there is an article on "How millions of Indian émigrés around the world are using their money and know-how to help their native land". We read of the Hindujas and the Harilelas.

Let us hope that Africans abroad who have acquired technical know-how and wealth will not only read this issue of *Business Week* but will emulate the patriotic examples of the Indians, Chinese and Jews of the Diaspora. Investing your savings in your country of origin manifests patriotism better than merely pontificating about the corruption or dictatorship at home. We who are here and are struggling to improve our country while accepting meagre rewards are not amused by our countrymen abroad who send us nothing but 'superior' ideas.

A genuine patriot is never tired of listening to John F. Kennedy: "Ask not what your country can do for you – ask what you can do for your country!" There is a lot waiting to be done, be assured of this, oh patriots at home and overseas!

12 November 1996

PUT IT IN THE SCHOOLS

Few students in schools these days could tell you who Dr Robert Laws was. Yet he was the prince of pioneer missionaries who brought into this country that Christian-cum-Western education which means so much to most of us these days.

The industrious Scotsman started his ventures at Cape Maclear in Mangochi in 1875, but later moved to Bandawe, Nkhata Bay (1881) and then Livingstonia, Rumphi (1894). By the end of the century he had dotted the whole of northern Malawi and eastern Zambia with village and central schools.

While economically and commercially northern Nyasaland was being laughed at as the dead north, educationally it was forging ahead marvellously. Dr Laws enthused the people up north with the Scottish love for education and excelling at examinations which has never flagged.

He was fond of quoting a German proverb, "What you would put into the nation put into the schools." Let this advice be adopted as food for our thoughts today. What is it we want for our nation, and how much of it are we putting into our schools?

As we cursorily wade through the history of nations and empires we see that education was provided for definite objectives. It was not gaining knowledge for its own sake. Basically it was intended to serve the nation and privileged individuals.

During ancient Greek and Roman times, education was confined to members of the ruling classes. Helots and plebeians just escorted the children of their masters to schools, but they themselves did not attend.

In 16th-century England it was being argued that education was only for the gentry who needed it for the purpose of governing the country. But by the 17th century some dissenting voices were saying that by denying the working classes the benefits of education, the country was being split into two nations: the nation of the cultured and rich on the one hand, and the nation of the poor and ignorant on the other hand.

When Christian missionaries came into this country, they were guided by the idea of Dr David Livingstone that Africans should be exposed to Christianity and legitimate commerce. The best-organised missionary societies did not therefore confine their work to Biblical lessons or church doctrine. They introduced industrial and commercial courses, agriculture, medicine, masonry and carpentry.

In the majority of cases, girls' education lagged behind that of boys, but not as a deliberate, official policy. On the contrary, right from the start missionaries used their wives or brought in lady missionaries to introduce literacy and domestic skills among African girls.

But the objectives for educating girls seemed more limited and less ambitious than those for boys. During my primary school days in the 1940s one would hear parents saying to their daughters: "Go to school and learn to read and write; educated men of today do not want to marry illiterate wives." Girls themselves could be heard saying: "I must learn to read and write so that when my husband writes me while he is working far away I can read the letters myself, instead of asking someone else to read them for me."

In those days it was not much emphasised that a girl had to get as much education as a boy in order to support herself. Rather she was being educated to be a helpmate to her husband. It was taken for granted then that every girl upon reaching a certain age would find a husband. Not so these days.

In this era of liberalisation in thought and enterprise, two questions need to be answered: who is to provide the education; the State or private agencies? What will be the objective of this education?

As to who is to provide education, one feels greatly persuaded by what Dr Ernest Baker of Oxford and King's College, London wrote: "I believe that the function of the State in education is to undertake work which would not be done at all if it were not undertaken by the State, but never to take over work which is already being undertaken unless that work is being done badly, and fails to reach the minimum standard of efficiency which the State is entitled and indeed bound to prescribe."

In short, the State should determine what should be taught in schools but not necessarily to provide all the schools. Private agencies may be involved, but what they teach there must be in consonance with national ideals and objectives.

Education must serve equally two purposes: making a citizen self-supporting and contributing to the common good.

That which we want to be in the nation let us first put it in our schools. Time and again our leaders have pleaded for national unity, and for us to forget our tribal divisions and quarrels of the past. We need to teach core subjects to all students regardless of their eventual careers. These core subjects should have as their aim the engendering in young people of nationhood, and the cherishing of altruism as against selfishness.

For example, as an aid to national unity our national language should be more intensively taught everywhere so that wherever two Malawians meet, here or abroad, they do not wonder in what language to greet each other or converse. Local dialects should, however, continue unhampered.

Secondary school teachers and students should not be confined to their districts or regions but assisted to teach or study anywhere. Our young people would then grow up to regard as a home a place where they live, work and make a living regardless of where they were born. What the Kansimas and Kampungas are advocating is wrong and must be rejected without reservations. Ethnic cleansing destroyed Yugoslavia, it will destroy Malawi.

A good citizen should be prepared to bargain for less than his due if in so doing the common good can be enhanced. It is appalling to hear well-educated people saying, "If they can award themselves 300 per cent increases, why should they not increase our salaries as much? If they do not increase our salaries by a hundred per cent we shall leave for greener pastures abroad."

Let us through core subjects inculcate in our young people that a great man insists on his rights at any cost, but a greater man renders his duties at any price. Democracy is a coin with two faces: one marked RIGHTS and another marked DUTIES. In schools both sides of the coin must be taught. You cannot prosper in an impoverished nation unless you help in improving it.

SONGS AND SORROWS ABOUT BOOKS

Francis Bacon (1561–1626) British lawyer, philosopher and member of Parliament wrote about the pleasure of reading and writing in words that have chimed musical chords over the ages. Said he, *inter alia*: "Some books are to be tasted, others to be swallowed and some few to be chewed and digested... Reading maketh a full man; conference a ready man; and writing an exact man."

He is a lucky youth who lives under the influence of a book-lover and self-educator. If he makes himself malleable to this mentor, he has the chance of becoming a somebody in life. All too often young people grow up in homes where bottles are more popular than books.

Citizens, read the biographies of great people: Tolstoy, Dickens, Churchill, Dunduzu Chisiza Sr, and others, and you will see how much reading after school days contributed to their intellect and success.

The education you get in school is a foundation on which to lay the marble pillar of true learning. He that stops reading the moment he gets his certificate or diploma brings upon himself the weeds and rust of ignorance. The certificate or diploma that he has, becomes to him like an oversized headgear. When we see someone wearing oversize clothes we suspect he has borrowed them, and who can blame us for thinking thus.

It is said the great American inventor Thomas Alva Edison attended school for only three months. He had to leave because his teachers regarded him as a dunce. But his mother had faith in the boy. She gave him extra lessons at home. To her delight, he devoured book after book that was placed in his hands.

To the benefit of mankind as a whole, Edison developed particular interest in science books or publications. He pored over the writings of Faraday, the British scientist, and turned Faraday's theories to inventions. Who can deny that the cinematograph, the gramophone and the electric lamp have enriched our quality of life. But Edison invented many more devices of civilisation.

At Britain's second most famous public school, Harrow, Winston Churchill disappointed his father and teachers. In his autobiography, *My Early Life*, he tells us that he loved and wanted to study English and History. His teachers required him to shine in the Classics (Greek and Latin) and Mathematics which he disliked. Their will prevailed against his. He failed again and again. For him the road to Oxford and Cambridge was closed.

But Churchill had an ambition. He knew that when one door is closed, the Lord opens another; you only have to look for it. While he was in India as a soldier he wrote his mother to send him Gibbon's *The Decline and Fall of the Roman Empire* and Adam Smith's *The Wealth of Nations*, as well as several other classics. He went ahead devouring the books, while practising the art of writing. You have to read only a few of his books to appreciate the benefits of reading after schooldays.

Whoever you are, whatever you are doing, you have a duty to yourself and your country to be better educated, better informed. The most prosperous countries in the world also have some of the best educated people. Highly educated people are seldom among the poorest. By highly educated people, I do not mean only those with multiple university degrees.

But what books must you read? This is the question that you should definitely ask yourself or someone. The market and libraries are brimful of books on all types of subjects. You cannot read all of them. Life is too short for such an undertaking. Just read the best books in your chosen field, be it science or humanities.

But what is a good book? Lord Bryce had this to say: "A book is good when it is bright and fresh, when it rouses and enlivens the mind, when it provides materials on which the mind can pleasurably work, when it leaves the reader not only knowing more but better able to use the knowledge he has received from it."

Life is a voyage through storms and blizzards. There are times when you find it easier to sigh than to smile. So many misfortunes rain upon you and you wonder: Was I put on this planet in order to suffer all these afflictions! At such occasions a good book may not cure you of the agony, physical or mental, but it can make you bear the thing with fortitude.

Every educated person should try to build up a library of his own. Some books are better owned than borrowed.

But how difficult it is these days to accumulate good books. The prices, huh! A book imported from India or Kenya will be more affordable than the one printed and published here. Malawi is a high-cost country in just about everything; no wonder we even have to buy imported pumpkins, cabbages and tomatoes rather than the local ones. But books are a must, a way to make them cheaper must be found. Expensive books discourage the habit of reading, and yet reading is a civilised habit.

Time and again I have stopped in front of a street vendor selling books on a variety of subjects, some looking filthy, others relatively clean. I have sometimes purchased a few of these, bearing imprints of reputable British and American publishers. The prices have been most affordable.

Whenever I have asked the vendor where he had obtained the books, all I have got is a knowing smile plus: "I bought them in Limbe." Then the vendor tries hard to divert me to another subject.

I used to feel good at obtaining some very good books at such bargain prices until one evening when I tried to reach for my favourite novel and re-read it, namely *Gone with the Wind* by Margaret Mitchell. It was not on my home shelf. Then I looked for Tolstoy's *The Cossacks*, and *Resurrection*. They were not there either.

A pause revealed that at least 200 of my books, including some which I have cherished since I was a schoolboy, were nowhere to be seen. Yes, my eyes could no longer fall on *My Years with General Motors* by A. Sloan, *Great Contemporaries* by Winston Churchill, *The Power of Positive Thinking* and other classics by Dr Norman Peale; an anthology on Voltaire, Emerson, the biography of Joseph Schumpeber by Swedenberg, and many others.

The other day I stopped in front of the former Malawi Book Service building and looked at the books on the ground there. With some difficulty I recognised a few of my missing books now looking as dirty as if they had been salvaged from a city of Blantyre refuse vehicle.

Every time you buy books from these street or verandah sellers, bear in mind that very likely someone is agonising about his vanished books. Apparently there is a highly educated crook in Blantyre or elsewhere who is invading bookstores, libraries, private homes and using the innocent, semi-literate vendors as his outlets.

Anyone reading today's column, who recognises some of the books I have cited above, should know I would be glad to ransom them from him. I am a man in sorrow. Books mean so much in my life.

24 June 1997

FROM SCOTLAND WITH LOVE

One of the plays staged in Blantyre recently that I would possibly have gone to see if I had heard of it was the one titled *Preacher Man*. It was reviewed in *The Nation* of 17 June 1997.

I understand it was about Dr David Livingstone, whose name needs no introduction to people in this part of Africa. Anybody who knows nothing about Dr Livingstone, possibly knows little else that a man of education generally knows.

I first heard of Dr Livingstone at the age of eight or nine during my second or third year as a village school pupil. Our teacher, whose enthusiasm for the name of Livingstone was perhaps greater than his knowledge, introduced Livingstone as a man sent to Africa by Jesus Christ. The dates as to when Livingstone and the disciples lived were not given. And if we thought Jerusalem and Nazareth were in Scotland it was not entirely our fault.

Well, Livingstone was not one of the 12 disciples, this is granted. But what was he? Opinions differ, especially in these post-colonial days when history books are undergoing revisionism. To the playwright of the play reviewed, Fletcher Ziwoya, Livingstone was a 'Preacher Man'. If I were able to write a play of my own of the life and work of Dr Livingstone it would possibly bear titles like 'From Scotland with Love', 'A Man of Compassion for the Unfortunate,' 'Pathfinder to the Heart of Africa'.

If we view Dr Livingstone as a mere preacher of the word of God as contained in the Bible, we will either be misrepresenting or underrating his work. For most of the three decades he spent in Africa he did little preaching, as preaching is conventionally understood.

Samuel Smiles, Livingstone's compatriot, in his classic book on success and achievers titled *Self-Help* writes: "In Africa Livingstone set to work with great zeal. He was not satisfied only with his own medical work, but he set himself other tasks, as well."

About the only African language Livingstone knew well enough to preach in was Sechuana, spoken in Botswana and the Transvaal. Whenever he was away from the tribes that spoke Sechuana, it is not clear how he could have done much preaching. He had African interpreters, but how much English did they know, and how well did they know languages other than those of their own tribes?

If we portray Livingstone as a mere preacher some would regard his work as nothing more than a museum piece. But when we view Dr Livingstone as a philosopher, guide and friend to our ancestors we find him and his work is still very relevant to us and our times. Some of the problems he found here in the 19th century are still around, such as man's inhumanity to man.

To a large extent Dr Livingstone was self-made. His parents were poor by British or European standards. His was not the wretchedness that we still see in African townships. When I visited the house in which he was born and brought up in Blantyre, Scotland, more than 30 years ago, I was amazed to see that it was a bungalow not unlike the ones senior African civil servants occupied in Naisi, Zomba.

From Livingstone's life we learn that poverty is not an insuperable barrier to success and fame in life. Those who are always pleading poverty as the reason why they cannot do this or that, are doing themselves an injustice.

Dr Livingstone was a man of strong determination. His first choice for a missionary field was China. When the door to China was closed, he turned to Africa. Down south where he started as an ordinary sedentary missionary, every morning as he peeped out of the window he could see clouds of smoke in the distance somewhere up north. "There must be more people there deserving contact," he thought.

As he visited those places, to his curiosity was added compassion for what he saw. Villages lying desolate, with human bodies rotting about, the work of slave traders. In the heart of Africa, especially on the shores of Lake Malawi, innocent people were being captured and sold to Swahili and Arab slave buyers.

When he asked Africans why they were engaging in destructive tribal wars, they told him they wanted to have cloth, guns and beads. The Swahilis and the Arabs would release these articles only in exchange for ivory. Slave vendors usually sold other people's children, not theirs.

He gave a lot of publicity to the evils of slave raiding and trading. He appealed to European, American and Turkish missionaries to come to Africa and introduce the message of love and hope. He was a man of compassion; and we still need such people.

But Livingstone had a practical approach to preaching. Mere homilies and sermons could not dissuade slave sellers from continuing with their diabolic export business. You had to show them that there was an alternative way of obtaining the calico and the hunting guns. After visiting a prominent African chief he would promise to send missionaries to his people, not just to preach the word of God but also to teach them how to grow crops like cotton for which manufacturers in Britain would readily offer their cloth to get. So came about Livingstone's formula of combating evil: Commerce and Christianity.

There is a message for us here too. We are presently very much baffled by rising crime and commercial sex. Punishment and preaching have their roles in arresting these social evils. However, increased opportunities for jobs and other honest means of earning a pile of kwachas would go a long way towards dissuading our youths from shameful deeds.

From Livingstone's life we learn the role of private initiative in the progress of nations. The decision to go into the interior of Africa was a private one. Neither Queen Victoria nor her Prime Minister had anything to do with it. The government came in much later. The missionaries who came to open their schools, hospitals and cathedrals found the means themselves. They did not ask for government subsidies, not at the beginning at any rate.

We have just learned that Malawi's place among the poorest of the poor countries has worsened. What is our reaction? We say, "It is the fault of those who ruled this country for three decades". Or we say, "Ah no, it is the fault of those who are in power now. They are incompetent and corrupt."

Such self-righteous claptrap may satisfy emotions but not empty stomachs; neither can it shield us from cold and ignorance. The responsibility for developing this country lies as much on the shoulders of private individuals as on officials. If you look at the history of developed countries like Britain, France, Germany, the United States and Japan, you will see that the wealth of those countries was generated mostly by private firms: by men like the Cadburys, Peugeots, Siemens, Henry Fords and Toyodas.

In his effort to fight the slave trade and to open Central Africa to Christianity and commerce, Livingstone risked his life. He was not discouraged when people told him of snakes, scorpions and savages waiting to end the life of any white man who ventured into the interior. The death of his wife at Shupanga, and one of his sons in the American Civil War naturally wounded him, but he stuck to his job with unflagging tenacity.

Without grit, pluck, tenacity or whatever other name you choose to mean perseverance, there can be no success. Malawi is a land of problems, gargantuan though not insuperable. But to turn it into a Switzerland, Denmark or Taiwan we have to adopt the right work ethic: work harder first before asking for higher rewards. And from Livingstone's life we learn that every job is worth doing.

WORK ETHIC AND HOLIDAYS

Adam and his wife Eve had been enjoying a life of plenty in the Garden of Eden till they offended God. In anger, the Lord said to Adam: "In the sweat of your face you shall eat bread till you return to the ground."

You do not have to be a pious person and to believe that there indeed was a couple called Adam and Eve. It is just important to recognise the fact that what we eat and drink comes from toiling and sweating. Anyone who eats and drinks without having worked first is doing so out of another person's labour.

We cannot have anything worthwhile unless we work for it. The greatest gift a parent can bequeath on his or her children is the love of work. Be fond of work and you keep at least half of the worries of life away.

The newspaper page that said the President had decreed holidays for all from Christmas to 5 January 1998, also reported the donor strictures on Malawi. We learned that Malawi, having performed poorly with the money donated to it, was to be penalised once more.

At the same time it was most galling to learn that nearly all Malawi's neighbours – Mozambique, Zambia and Tanzania – had performed to the satisfaction of the donors. What went awry with Malawi? What must we do to make Malawi a more prosperous country? A one-paragraph or one-sentence answer may conceal realities. However, it may contain a seed out of which a baobab tree of success could emerge.

Let us once more prick up our ears and listen to the great American, the man whose wisdom and influence played a decisive role in making the United States a nation of great achievers. I am referring to Benjamin Franklin (1706–90).

When some people asked him how he had managed to become wealthy, he replied: "In short, the way to wealth, if you desire it, is as plain as the way to market. It depends chiefly on two words: Industry and Frugality i.e. waste neither time nor money, but make the best use of both. He that gets all he can honestly, and saves what he gets (necessary expenses excepted) will certainly become rich if that Being who governs the world, to whom all should look for a Blessing in their honest endeavours, doth not in his wise Providence otherwise determine."

What the American sage said is as applicable to an individual's quest for self-improvement as to that of a nation. In this article, it is on our national economic problems that we should try to reason together.

Are we really working hard? Perhaps it depends on how one defines the phrase working hard. Whatever else it may mean, working hard has to do with working until one completes the day's task. There are people who think they have worked hard on a particular day if they have arrived on time, say 7.30 am and left on time, say 5 pm. Hard work must be measured by the output and quality of the work.

We are living in an age when some work ethics conceived in international organisations do us more harm than good.

In developed countries there is continuous pressure to reduce the length of a working day or week. Some people there would reduce a working day from eight hours to seven hours, and five days a week to four.

Some labour leaders and socialists in Africa may advocate similar practices here. But we must not forget that when Europe and America were undergoing industrial revolutions, people there were working from dawn to dusk.

As those countries invented labour-saving machines, it was possible for workers to stay in factories less time and yet to manufacture more goods. When the working day was reduced to ten hours it was seen as a great improvement.

In developing countries most of our work is done manually and this makes it necessary that we stay on the job each day longer and have fewer holidays annually than in developed countries.

How did Japan and the other Tigers of the Far East come to challenge the industrialised west? They worked harder and consumed less when they were a good deal poorer than Europe and America.

The jealous leaders damned Japanese factories as 'sweat shops', but the Japanese, the Taiwanese and the South Koreans went on. We all know the results.

How many holidays do we need a year in Malawi? The fewer the better. Whoever conceived the idea of giving employees holidays throughout the Christmas and New Year period misfired.

This is not the way to Malawi's prosperity. We must not waste time in 'resting', otherwise hunger and disease will overtake us. Recently, civil servants have constantly gone on strike; just what extra rest did they need?

Malawians, countrymen, do we seriously want to achieve higher standards of living. If so let us re-read what Benjamin Franklin said and be guided by him. Deficits take place in the government budget because people there forget that for Malawi to achieve affluence, 'industry and frugality' must be embraced simultaneously.

REFLECTIONS ON THE 1999/2000 BUDGET

Malawi is a member of two major economic groupings, SADC and COMESA. These economic blocs have as their objective free trade. Free trade is an ideal that is usually advocated by countries and firms that are already in a strong enough position to compete. Malawi's industry base is still embryonic and fragile. Any reduction in tariffs should be taken step by step. Taiwan and South Korea threw their markets open after their industries had grown beyond the infant stage. The European Economic Community (EEC) was launched in 1957. Complete reduction of tariffs took place over a period of more than two decades. France was particularly protective of its agricultural industry.

If our standards of living are to improve comfortably we must go in for manufacturing on a grand scale. But how do we go about it? Perhaps we should find out how the Tigers of the Far East managed to achieve a high level of industrialisation within a period of 30 to 40 years.

Recently I had the opportunity to talk to some Chinese officials from the Republic of China, Taiwan. They denied that what they had achieved in Taiwan was a miracle, because a miracle is something of a mystery which cannot be explained. They said things started going in the right direction when their government made up its mind to see industries established in Taiwan. To facilitate this, education was made compulsory, and now illiteracy has been eliminated. Vocational training was intensified to provide industries with skilled labour; the government acted as a 'baby-sitter' to the infant industries that private firms established; crime was checked while foreign investment was encouraged. Crowning it all, the people worked extra hard.

Agriculture is the mainstay of the Malawi economy. Though its full potential has not yet been realised, without a healthy agricultural base the rest of the economy cannot tick. And yet we must not stake everything on agriculture if we are really serious about taking Malawi into the family of middle-income countries. Malawi must aggressively embark on industrialisation. Agricultural exports are not quite income-elastic. As our traditional customers earn more and more income they do not proportionately spend more money on our exports.

They spend their extra incomes on the products of manufacturing industries. Like Taiwan, South Korea and Thailand, we too should venture into manufacturing. But why are we not doing so already? The basic problem in Malawi is the absence of a class of people who are not afraid of business risks; people with a high propensity to save and invest rather than to consume. The government must take calculated steps to breed and nurture such a class of people, the entrepreneurs.

Of course, we should throw the doors of our country open so that foreign entrepreneurs may come in and set up their industries. Already we have provided generous incentives. All the same, we have not experienced an avalanche of investments yet. In the world of today investment opportunities are looking for business people rather than business people looking for investment opportunities. Potential investors do not just look at Malawi's offers in isolation. They compare what we offer with what others offer, and they do not seem to find us very attractive. So what are we to do? Maybe we should offer still more incentives such as tax holidays, but we may be sacrificing too much for nothing.

The ways of successful individual entrepreneurs elsewhere in the world may suggest what we should do when foreign investors are not responding to our invitations. John H. Johnson of *Ebony* magazine used to canvass for support from the wealthy people he knew. But more often than not he did not receive the help he needed. Later he wrote in his autobiography. "When I had exhausted every avenue of support, I returned to Johnson rule Number one ... what can you by yourself do with what you have to get what you want? And I made some interesting discoveries."

Government, while selling some of its corporations to private owners, ought to reserve the right to start new ones or buy back those which after being taken up by private firms are not operating in the interest of the economy as a whole.

Imagine, for example, a firm that has been manufacturing products using local materials and employing hundreds of local people, bought by a foreign company which then transforms it into a mere selling agency for products manufactured in another country. Can we truly say that privatisation in this case has served a national purpose? I agree with those who advise the government to proceed cautiously about privatising Admarc.

We have sometimes heard conflicting news about the state of lendable funds in the country. Some people have warned the Government that its propensity to borrow from lending institutions is elbowing out private borrowers.

But other public relations executives have said there are abundant funds waiting for borrowers and that not many people are coming forward.

Presumably the terms are beyond the capability of those in need of loans. As my Swahili friend told me *'Kama huna pesa, hupate pesa'*. If you do not have money, you cannot have money! In other words, to have a loan, you must already be a man of property. But how many Malawians are in that position?

It is here perhaps that the government can help by adopting entrepreneurial policies and attitudes. There should be venture capital: that is capital which will be disbursed on the basis of "If you do not dare, you won't be there!" Government should create a fund out of which to grant loans to persons who seem to have the potential for business success even if they do not have a pile of kwacha of their own already. Those who think this is foolhardy should recall what Queen Isabella I and her husband Ferdinand of Spain did. A penniless sailor called Christopher Columbus approached them as a last resort for support in a venture he wanted to make. He believed he could reach India and China and do business there by sailing on the Atlantic westwards. Other kings of Europe had dismissed Columbus as a hopeless dreamer. But Isabella and Ferdinand granted Columbus venture capital in the form of six ships and a number of sailors. That was in 1492. In October that year Columbus discovered a continent that soon made Spain fabulously rich.

It is up to us as a nation to take bold decisions if we want to transform Malawi from a wretched country to a prosperous one. If we keep on doing things the same way year in, year out we will remain the same country, over-populated and indigent.

<u>7 April 2000</u>

LESSONS FROM MALAWI'S ECONOMIC HISTORY

The modern economic history of Malawi begins with the arrival of resident missionaries from Scotland. Their forerunner David Livingstone had advocated the introduction of commerce and Christianity simultaneously, as a means of conquering the evils of ignorance and the slave trade.

Our society at the time Livingstone visited us was semi-open to external influences. For several centuries most tribes in the present Malawi were being visited by foreigners who came to buy ivory, leopard and lion skins. These they took to the east coast of Africa where they exchanged them for clothes, beads and guns from the Arabs and the Portuguese. In the course of time, some of these traders from the east coast came to buy slaves as well. We can describe the economy of Malawi at that time as extractive. Our ancestors extracted the natural resources of the country mostly from forestry. We do not hear that there was any sort of mining. There was hardly any fishing for export.

The period 1875 to 1895 saw the intensification of extractive industries. Europeans entered this country with powerful guns. The Moir brothers, John and Fred, engaged in much elephant poaching. Alfred Sharpe, later to become Commissioner after Henry Johnston, and Captain Frederick Lugard, future Governor General of Nigeria, came to this country in the 1880s to seek fortunes in ivory hunting. Even after he had retired as Governor, Sharpe came back to continue hunting. Whenever they defeated Yao Chiefs like Makanjira and Zerafi (Jalasi) Johnston and Sharpe seized the ivory they found in the chief's stockades and then exported it. In 1891, when this country became a British Protectorate, ivory constituted 80 per cent of its exports.

In the 1870s, whenever missionaries like John Buchanan of the Church of Scotland visited villages on the Shire Highlands, they found Mang'anja men engaged in cotton spinning and weaving, while others made bark clothes which earned Buchanan's admiration. At the same time cheap Manchester calico was imported into the country. Within 10 years the village textile industries died. Nearly 80 years had to pass before Malawians were to acquire weaving and spinning skills again under David Whitehead and Sons. The disappearance of domestic textile weaving was not lamented by the new rulers of the country. British economic policy since the era of the American colonies was that colonies were to produce raw materials and export them to England. Factories in Britain would transform the raw materials to manufactured goods which would then be exported to the colonies. In this way, it was said, the colonial system benefited the colony and the 'mother' country alike.

In 1879 Henry Henderson brought 56 lbs of Liberian coffee to the mission station which now bears his name in Blantyre. Out of this package only seven plants survived. But that was the beginning of what in a few years was to become a flourishing coffee industry. In 1893 coffee ranked second to ivory as Malawi's main export. By the year 1900 coffee constituted 80 per cent of exports. But soon after it was to head for a decline from which it was never to recover fully. This was because between the years 1895 and 1905 Brazil doubled its production of coffee and flooded the world market with its exports. Coffee prices tumbled below costs of production. Because of this reason as well as drought, disease and shortages of labour, coffee as a cash crop became unprofitable and was abandoned in favour of tea, tobacco and cotton.

Coffee growing was a predominantly European and large estate industry. This was in contrast with the approach in Uganda and Tanganyika (around Mount Kilimanjaro). Professor Bridglal Pachai concludes his account of the history of coffee growing in Malawi by saying "In its short history the rise and fall of the coffee industry had many lessons to teach. Firstly, planters in a new country should not place their hopes on a single crop; the success of local industry depended upon judicious use of land and labour resources, in both of which the early planters made serious mistakes. Greater productivity demanded that the majority of the people, in this case Africans, should be more closely involved in production as producers in their own right rather than as observers and labourers."

What Professor Pachai says is supported by the history of coffee in the economies of Uganda and Tanzania. The Baganda and the Chagga prospered growing coffee on their peasant farms. Whatever price fluctuations their coffee exports suffered on international markets, they did not ruin the growers as they cultivated other crops for their food.

In Malawi, the white farmers strongly objected to allowing Africans to grow coffee, and for that matter, tea. Yet if the growing of coffee in Malawi had been entrusted to smallholders, as in Uganda and Tanzania, it too would have weathered the Brazilian price effects.

A lesson for our times is that wherever possible, the growing of a cash crop should be popularised instead of restricted to a few. In times of prosperity, many benefit and see no need of flocking to jobless urban areas. In times of world price recessions, the burden is shouldered by many and is less crushing.

The missionaries who brought coffee seedlings also brought tea seedlings. Before Europeans came, people in many parts of Malawi were already growing cotton, especially in the Lower Shire and Karonga. They were also growing tobacco everywhere. However, it was the European planters with the assistance of the government who introduced cotton and tobacco on the world market. They knew world markets better than Malawians did.

John Buchanan first arrived in this country as a missionary with the title of gardener. Today we would call him by the more dignified term of horticulturalist. He was dismissed because of his violence in handling African servants. Yet this man perhaps more than any other planter deserves our thanks for promoting the growing of cash crops that are still with us today.

After the disappearance of coffee, more and more farmers turned to the growing of tea and tobacco. For some years tea was Malawi's main export. Indeed during colonial days Malawi used to boast of being the largest tea grower in Africa and the third in the British Empire. But eventually in Malawi tobacco overtook tea, and in Africa Kenya overtook Malawi as a producer of tea. You have to keep on increasing your speed just to remain where you are.

By quickly resorting to the production of tea, tobacco and cotton, the planters and the Government saved the Malawi economy after the coffee industry had collapsed. Now that the tobacco industry is under a death sentence pronounced by the World Health Organisation, we must act with even greater speed. The country must diversify, not only within the agricultural sector but throughout the whole economy. How? This is a big subject on its own, requiring a separate essay.

26 June 2000

ECONOMIC CONSEQUENCES OF DEMOCRACY

On 21 June 2000 I had the privilege of attending the pre-budget consultative forum organised by the Ministry of Finance and Economic Planning in conjunction with the Malawi Investment Agency. I came back intellectually refreshed, but at the same time aghast that there is much awareness of the causes of our economic backwardness, and yet so little of this knowledge has been used to accelerate the development of our beloved country.

Though democracy accords people freedom of choice, not many would prefer poverty to wealth. As George Bernard Shaw put it, where there is no money you have ignorance, poverty and disease. No one loves a life of ill-health.

It was startling to learn that at the time Malawi was getting its independence, its per capita income was higher than that of Singapore and Taiwan. Both of these countries, geographically smaller than Malawi, are now prosperous countries by international standards. They have left us far behind. What did people there and in Mauritius do that we have not done?

From the debates and interventions that took place at the forum, I got the impression that lack of capital and inadequate skills are only some of the handicaps that retard economic development.

Sociological and psychological factors also deserve attention. We have readily taken to the material products of developed and wealthy countries, but have not yet accepted the sacrifices that are the preconditions of attaining higher living standards.

The great German sociologist Max Weber (1864–1920) explained the extraordinary success of minority religious groups in Europe like the Calvinists, Nonconformists and Quakers in terms of what he called the Protestant ethic. Whether Protestantism had anything to do with the ethic is debatable in view of similar achievements in recent decades made in other parts of the world where Protestantism has had no impact. Weber noted that those people believed in hard work, frugality and risk taking. To the Calvinists, success in business was seen as evidence of blessings from God. It was exemplified in America by Benjamin Franklin, who saw the road to wealth as made up by two things: industry and frugality, plus God's blessing.

Before people can fully commit themselves to developing their countries, there must be a kind of spiritual experience. They must feel that success in material wealth is something worth toiling for. They must be emotionally charged and prepared to stand up to the hardships that are inevitable on the road to economic success.

In Malawi, we need to remind ourselves that there is no gain without pain, and that he that is to reap the harvest is the one who must do the ploughing. There is a limit to the extent people of other countries will pay taxes to their respective governments, for them to donate some of the proceeds to the people of Malawi who need cheap fertilisers or famine relief.

Passing on such a message to the people in a democratic Malawi is not easy. Some people think democracy means an easy life. If you voted somebody to power, he owes you a living, and if he forgets to make good his promises, you must blackmail him by saying next time you will vote for his rival.

Just imagine two men canvassing for votes. One says to the people: If you vote for me, I will go and ask Parliament to build you a road here so that you can easily take your produce to the market. But make sure you work harder in the field to justify the existence of such a road. Another says I will go and ask Parliament first to build a road and then bring you food on the road to supplement your own meagre harvest. You do not have to toil harder. People will prefer the second candidate. They do not like someone who faces reality with honesty and candour. They do not vote for the man who talks the language of Winston Churchill, that if we are to avert defeat, we must be prepared to sweat tears and blood.

To accelerate development, people at all levels of society must be willing to accept the necessary sacrifices. Just about everyone nowadays says that the civil service has become less dedicated to duty than before. But why is this so? Why has morale or professionalism gone downhill?

During the two previous regimes, everyone of working age who was physically fit was required to make a contribution to the national budget. Those not working or earning very little used to pay poll taxes. To suggest that the poll tax be reinstated would not be wise in the politics of today. But to ease pressure on the budget, there is no reason why the government, having undertaken not to charge fees in primary schools, should not ask parents to buy pencils and exercise books for their children. Everyone who brings a child into this world has a duty to see that he or she educates that child. The role of the government is to support parental responsibilities, but not replace them.

Political leaders should take part in reorienting people away from a dependency culture to one of self-reliance. Trying to win or retain office by encouraging people to live idle lives is unworthy of anyone who poses as a leader. In the richest countries of the world, people have learnt to discipline themselves rather than be disciplined by the State or by starvation. They work and work, save and save. They cherish a work ethic that is conducive to economic development. There is no other path to development.

In short, I would say I came back from the forum convinced as never before that the resources of manpower and material are already within our country's borders. We just have to reorganise ourselves for greater effort. We cannot make much progress without an honest, dedicated and patriotic civil service. The civil servants, at least those in the upper segment, know more than the rest of us just how much money the government can afford to spare for salaries. So what are their grievances? Candour is called for here. When we talk of government, we mean not just a few cabinet ministers, but the whole civil service as well.

11 July 2000

WHY READ BIOGRAPHIES?

Reading for pleasure or profit is not as popular a pastime in Malawi as watching soccer. Most of the young ones who read books have examinations in mind. However, many of those who read books are not voracious readers of biographies. This is a pity.

Both the reading and writing of biographies is very popular in America and Britain. Everyone who makes a name in a certain field, be it science, literature or politics, will usually have a book written about him or her. Thomas Carlyle (1795–1881), Scottish historian and man of letters, defined history as innumerable biographies. He saw the history of a nation as made up of the biographies of its heroes.

No doubt there is a point in this. Who can read the biography of Winston Churchill without getting a good glimpse of British history during the two world wars? Who can read the biography of Jomo Kenyatta without having a fair idea of Kenya's march to independence, or that of Kamuzu Banda without learning about the Federation of Rhodesia and Nyasaland and much more?

People who read biographies do so because they are looking for information about how someone achieved greatness. Reading a biography is like passing through a thick forest; you see, hear and find out more than you expected, and quite often, what you come across is pretty startling.

Usually we know people only after they have achieved fame or wealth. Little do we know the hurdles that they overcame. Many of us have heard of how Churchill bravely led Britain and its empire to victory. But few of us know that at certain times during the war there was talk of removing him. He reveals this in Volume Four of his book, *The Second World War*, where he writes: "I had now been 28 months at the head of affairs during which we had sustained an almost unbroken series of military defeats. There followed a long catalogue of my failures and a wealth of proposals for lightening my burdens by taking power out of my hands." This is Churchill's understatement.

Somewhere in his writings Churchill says that if you want to succeed, never ever give up the struggle. And this is what he did himself. In the face of defeats he kept on urging his nation to stand firm, to fight in the air, to fight on the seas, to fight anywhere until the enemy 'gets enough of it'. To many people Thomas Alva Edison, the inventor of electric light, the phonograph and many other modern wonders, was a rare genius. But from his biographies we learn that Edison described genius as 99 per cent perspiration and only one per cent inspiration. From other biographies we learn that genius is nothing but the capacity to take infinite pains.

Students in primary schools in Malawi and other British colonies during the period up to the 1950s were exposed to the study and reading of biographies. They were taught about great Africans like Shaka, founder of the Zulu nation, Moshoeshoe of the Sutu, John Tengo Jabavu, co-founder of Fort Hare University College, Apolo Kagwa of Uganda and Dr James Kwegyir Aggrey of Gold Coast (Ghana).

Why this part of the history syllabus had to be dropped I have not found out. But it was a mistake to do so. It is not enough that students of physics learn that it was Newton who propounded the Law of Gravity. They should be taught his methods and life as a scientist. From John Maynard Keynes's profile of Isaac Newton we learn that his "peculiar gift was the power of holding continuously in his mind a purely mental problem until he had seen straight through it". This is another way of saying Newton had strong powers of concentration. You cannot succeed as a scientist or anything else if you allow your mind or interests to wander.

From the biographies of Charles Darwin, Louis Pasteur and Albert Einstein we learn that at school they had not been very bright students; in later life they were to achieve so much. If at school your grades were mediocre do not be discouraged. Now concentrate on a field that interests you. One day you might wake up to find yourself among the great achievers of your generation.

Teaching of biography should be reintroduced in schools, while general reading of biographies should be encouraged. When you have read the biography of a great person you find your own life enriched.

<u>2 October 2000</u>

THE ROLE OF THE STATE IN ECONOMIC GROWTH

In this age of globalisation, every country that is development-conscious is in competition with other countries near and far for capital investment and markets.

Dr Peter F. Drucker, the American management guru, calls this age the age of knowledge. Success in commercial and economic endeavours tends to be assured where people have the requisite knowledge for managing affairs. Since we are in competition with the rest of the world, the level of our knowledge, information and technology has to be comparable with that of our main competitors. Those who are indolent in the acquisition of knowledge should not expect the rest of the world to spare them the competition.

A good deal of the knowledge we need for the management of our economic and social programmes can be gleaned out of publications of such well-staffed international bodies as the World Bank and the IMF. Unfortunately, they do not seem to be readily available to the public at large here in Malawi. Visit bookshops, you find none. It is only recently that, by chance, I came across a very valuable publication called *World Development Report* 1997. It discusses the role of the State in a changing world.

Some of the economic problems facing us are not adequately being solved because we have not clarified the roles of the State and private firms as well as individuals in the management of the economy. With the end of World War II in the industrialised countries, there was consensus that the State could manage most major industries better than privately owned firms. It was for this reason that in Britain the Labour Government of Clement Attlee nationalised major industries, including the Bank of England.

In newly independent states of Africa, where few major industries existed, they were immediately nationalised. For example, Zambia's Copperbelt industries. Where no major industries existed, the independent State set about launching its own industries. Dr Nkrumah of Ghana set the example, not only in gaining independence but also in establishing State enterprises.

Several decades later, both in industrialised and development countries, first economists and later politicians began attributing their countries' lacklustre performance in international trade to the incompetence of State-run enterprises. They were seen as over-staffed and mismanaged by political party favourites. Then came the age of Thatcherism, when State enterprises were sold en masse to private entrepreneurs.

These industrialised countries then took the gospel of privatisation to developing countries. In giving loans or grants, they insisted that the developing country should liberalise its economy and sell State enterprises.

What is the ideal or commendable role of the State in an economy? Since State ownership of enterprises has been rejected, is the management of the economy to be left entirely to the whims of private entrepreneurs? The 1997 World Bank Report says, "the message of experience since then is rather different: the State is central to economic and social development, not as a direct provider of growth but as a partner, catalyst and facilitator."

What does it mean in the Malawian context? Occasionally I stop at supermarkets to buy a chicken from the freezer and ask whether the chicken is from a local farm. Invariably, I am told that it is imported, and that the shop buyer cannot find local suppliers.

This sounds odd when, soon after leaving the shop, I meet a man carrying a large basket full of brown-feathered chickens, offering them for sale to anyone who looks as if he is interested. Every weekend, I go to the Ndirande market and there I see lots of chickens in cages waiting for buyers. The supply appears to be greater than the demand.

Here is where the State could come in. It need not set up chicken farms of its own, but it could do something to facilitate communication between the breeders and the buyers. How? Well, go and find out just what is the real problem at the moment.

The report says that if the State is to play an effective role in an economy, its capability must be strengthened. "In successful countries," goes the report, "policy-making has been embedded in consultative processes which provide civil society, labour unions and private firms opportunities for input and oversight".

State institutions should be reinvigorated by, amongst other things, providing public servants with the incentive to perform better and to shun bribery and corruption. Appointments and promotions should be based on merit. State capability and effectiveness must be enhanced. "The two – good policies and more capable State institutions to implement – produce faster economic development. People living with ineffective States have long suffered consequences."

The minimalist State, where the State does little or nothing, is a tragedy. See what transpired in Liberia and Somalia when the State withered.

On the other hand, small improvements in the State's effectiveness lead to higher standards of living, in turn paving the way for more reforms and further development.

The trouble in Malawi is that political parties have done little theorising on matters like the role of the State in the economy. The liberalised market economy was adopted with some prompting from donors because State businesses had become insolvent. When State intervention was introduced about 60 years ago, the argument was that the market could not be trusted to deliver the goods. So somewhere a line must be drawn. For example, when the kwacha continues to depreciate, what must the government do about it? At present, newspaper reports forecast currency depreciation with some resignation, or just condemn the monetary authorities as if they were exclusively responsible for everything that is going wrong in the economy. Who is wasting scarce reserves by importing tomatoes and eggs from abroad? Must the State just *'laissez-faire'* or take corrective measures?

23 October 2000

TIPS THAT COULD TILT THE ECONOMY

Pain, whether physical or mental, makes different people react in ways that are diametrically opposed. This may be due to their natural makeup or something else. We have heard the saying: necessity is the mother of invention. When some people are facing extreme hardships they think out new ideas of doing things. Sometimes they find the solution. The great economist John Maynard Keynes wrote his masterpiece, *The General Theory of Employment Interest and Money,* to try and rescue British and world economies from the devastating effects of the Great Depression which started in 1929 with the New York stock market crash. Economic hardships of this sort elsewhere brought about *coups d'état*, dictatorships or civil wars.

Pestilences have compelled some people in certain countries to investigate causes of disease and find cures. In other countries at other times such situations have given rise to witch-hunting. People have not bothered to find out the real causes of their health problems. They may just assume that it is that childless, ugly-looking woman who is wreaking vengeance on the community.

Elements of both the quiet scientific investigator and the hysterical witch-hunter are very much with us today. While some persons are spending half their nights trying to find solutions to the economic agonies of this country, others have already concocted short-cut remedies; sent to the gallows corrupt ministers and civil servants. It is their corrupt ways that have made us all dirt poor.

There is no doubt that witches and cannibals have at one time or another been the source of suffering, just as at present persons who engage in bribery and corruption are undoubtedly contributing to the sickness of the economy. But what is required of us is deeper thinking and deeper reasoning to find out if there are other causes of our wretchedness. It may give consolation to one's ego to know or believe that one's poverty is the fault of other people, such as the rich nations who refuse to write off our debts. It is wiser to listen to Socrates the Greek philosopher when he says "know yourself."

In the way people write about the sliding kwacha, one would get the impression that the currency is the sole cause of our suffering. But actually, the kwacha is to the economy what a clinical thermometer is to a hospital patient.

When the thermometer shows a patient's temperature is below or above normal, the fault is not in the thermometer, but in the body. No matter what you do to the thermometer, this will not make the patient's temperature return to normal.

In other words, let us focus our thoughts and actions on the elements of the economy: the agricultural sector from which we get food and cash crops, the export sector which brings us such necessary conveniences as clothes, medicines, books and the building industry which is the source of our shelters. What can we do to these various sectors that will give us more of what we need and want?

Once these sectors give us more, you will see the kwacha stabilising *vis-à-vis* other currencies. If the kwacha now fares badly when positioned against major currencies of the world, especially the dollar, this simply means our economy is too weak compared with the economies of other countries.

What are we to do? And how should we do it? The other day as I was about to board the coachline to Lilongwe, I met two gentlemen of the type that give scientific thought to our economic situation. "Why is the Malawi economy not growing faster?" we asked each other. Instead of the three of us laying all the blame on the people who occupy high positions, we debated the influences of culture. Some economists writing on the economics of developing countries have urged that unless Africans give up some of their customs and adapt to western customs, they will never experience the industrialisation that the west has achieved. We noted, however, that the Japanese and the Indians have achieved a lot of economic success without giving up their traditional values. Why then should African culture be inimical to economic development? Without advocating wholesale repudiation of African culture, we agreed that certain aspects of it ought to be given up. We lamented the custom whereby, if one member of a family gets a good job or succeeds in business, other members of the extended family stop trying to make their own little pile and just sponge on their relative. Have you seen Asian children in shops, how they handle customers? No wonder the family wealth keeps on increasing even after the founder of the firm grows infirm or passes away.

The other day I was chatting with one of the well-travelled men from the cold Northern Hemisphere. When I expressed the concern that we have about the impending collapse of our tobacco industry, he told me he had lived in Sri Lanka, a country whose economy formerly depended on one crop, tea, as ours is on tobacco. Now, he said, despite the civil wars, the people of Sri Lanka have diversified their economy. Apart from framing industrial policies that are conducive to foreign investment, the Sri Lankans have acquired a variety of skills. A foreign investor is able to hire highly-skilled local people at wages that make it possible for his products to compete in world markets. "Do you know," said the good gentleman, "in India you can find people who are poorer than the poor people you see here. Yet India's middle class population is bigger than that of Germany." I gasped with wonder, having lived in Deutschland for three years and having learned to say *'Guten Morgen.'* Is there something we can learn from people in Sri Lanka and those in India? I believe there is a lot. The sure way to remain backward and poor is to resist change.

Do you know what some potential investors are saying? They say Mozambique is more business-friendly than Malawi. They say in Beira that when you apply for a business licence you get it in a matter of days. In Blantyre they say officials keep you waiting for the better part of a year.

It is effective handling of matters such as I have raised above that could provide the country with a bootstrap. What the central bank can do to stabilise the kwacha will only act as a palliative, not a permanent cure.

20 November 2000

WHERE DEMOCRACY RETARDS GROWTH

Provide one country with capital goods and schools, it prospers. We find examples of such a country in Asia's Far East. Provide another country with the same capital and schools, it gets poorer. You find such examples in Africa. Indeed, some African countries are poorer now than they were under colonial rule 40 years ago. Why?

Part of the answer may be found in the philosophy of Bertrand Russell. In an essay titled *Reconciliation of individuality and citizenship*, he wrote, *inter alia*, "when the authorities are also stupid (which may occur), they will tend to side with the stupid children and acquiesce, at least tacitly, in rough treatment for those who show intelligence. In that case, a society will be produced in which all the important positions will be won by those whose stupidity enables them to please the herd. Such a society will have corrupt politicians, ignorant schoolmasters, policemen who cannot catch criminals and judges who condemn innocent men. Such a society, even if it inhabits a country full of natural wealth, will in the end grow poor from inability to choose able men for important posts. Such a society, though it may prate of Liberty and even erect statues in her honour, will be a persecuting society which will punish the very men whose ideas might save it from disaster."

Can we see our African face in this statement as clearly as in a mirror? At least some of us may join Abebayo Williams of Nigeria who laments about his country (*Africa Today*, October 2000). "Imagine a country uniquely blessed with human resources and impossibly gifted individuals but which elects certificate forgers and fourth-rate pedestrians as its pathfinders… How did a nation with so much possibility manage to squander its rich human and natural resources!"

Nigeria is not alone in this economic and social debacle. Britain left Ghana, Uganda and Zambia with prosperous economies and ample foreign reserves. Belgium left Congo (Kinshasa) rich in copper and diamonds. In all these countries, people have experienced harder times than they had experienced under colonial rule.

Britain did not leave Malawi with an ample dowry. But towards the late 1960s and the beginning of the 1970s, for a variety of reasons, Malawi was performing economically so well as to receive approving remarks from international aid donors. There was a time indeed when Malawi had ample resources. Unfortunately, sooner than later, these resources vanished.

In search for the route to prosperity, we must not shy away from self-criticism. The culture of a society determines, to a very great extent, whether a country will benefit from the resources it has and those it gets from donors.

Because of the desire to enhance popularity with the people, a government has sometimes diverted funds from investment to consumption, from projects with long gestation periods to ones with shorter periods just to placate the voting crowd.

It was a noble intention for a government to launch a State enterprise for the purpose of providing goods and services as well as employment. But the desire for popularity meant staffing these enterprises with the nice guys rather than the most capable ones. As a result, most State employees became white elephants in the economy.

It is nice to establish financial institutions that lend money on subsidised interest. But the borrowers must be capable of making productive use of the money and repaying it. It is no music to hear someone saying, "Why should I pay back this loan, after all I voted correctly. This is my reward."

Just as it is from a small seed that a giant tree grows, so it is from the bite of a tiny mosquito that a hefty six foot giant dies. What can benefit the economy and what can destroy starts as a minute thing. While democracy means serving and pleasing people, we must not hesitate to remind ourselves that even the Lord who created us has taken us some way, not the whole way to abundance. He has sent us the rains, but left us to do the hoeing. We must accept the fact that even under democracy, people have to make sacrifices. The only difference with sacrifices you make under dictatorship is that under democracy the rewards go to the toiler, under dictatorship the fruits are reaped by the slave master.

Democracy retards economic development when it is 'populist' and inclined to pander to people's base desires. What did you say Benjamin Franklin? Oh please remind us: "The way to prosperity, if you desire it, is as clear as the road to the market. It consists of two words: industry (hard work) and frugality."

President Hastings Banda admonished Malawians to work hard in the fields but he was taciturn on the other necessity, frugality. I remember at one time he received applause at the stadium that bore his name when he said "Why should we not spend the money. You don't take it with you to heaven."

President Bakili Muluzi also appeals to his people to work harder. But he should also be appealing to them about frugality, which entails spending wisely or else putting aside money until it is needed.

LESSONS FROM ADAM SMITH

During the medieval years of European history (AD 1000 to 1500) some scholars delved into the great literary, philosophical and scientific works of the previous Greek and Roman ages which they had long put away and neglected. They re-read the works of such Greek sages as Aristotle and Plato, read the works of the Fathers of the Church, Augustine of Hippo, Ambrose and Gregory, and the more recent works of Copernicus, Thomas Aquinas. This process gathered momentum and it gave birth to the Renaissance. Henceforth, Europe became the world's leading continent on this planet.

As we read the works of modern authorities in science and literature, it sometimes pays to delve into the works of bygone days which are often cited by modern writers but rarely read by anyone. Instead of going through works of modern Nobel Prize laureates in economics like Paul Samuelson and Milton Friedman, I decided to peep into Adam Smith's legendary work, *The Wealth of Nations*. What does he say about nations trying to emerge from poverty to prosperity?

Our central concern in Malawi today is poverty eradication. This is a noble goal indeed, but it can only be attained in conditions of accelerated economic growth. Over several decades, the growth rate of the GDP in Malawi has only been marginally higher than the demographic growth rate. No wonder, improvements in standards of living have been barely perceptible.

What does Adam Smith say about economic growth? Alternatively, what hints does he throw which can help us in searching for the route to economic growth? We may profitably examine what the great 18th-century Scotsman says about division of labour, markets, capital and productive labour.

The most obvious evidence of economic growth is the increase in the quantity of goods and the quality thereof. For such growth and improvement to take place, there must be division of labour. Smith had this to say, "The great increase of the quantity of work which, in consequence of the division of labour, the same number of men are capable of performing is owing to three different circumstances. First, to the increase of dexterity in every particular workman; secondly, to the saving of time which is commonly lost in passing from one species of work to another; and lastly, to the invention of a great number of machines which facilitate and abridge labour and enable one man to do the work of many."

In rural Malawi, production of goods is at a low level because there is not much division of labour. Traditionally, there is division of labour between males and females. But apart from division based on gender, every man tends to be a Jack of all trades. He cultivates the fields, erects the barn wherein to store his maize, he carves hoe handles, he hunts, he catches fish. Above all, he builds his own hut. In the past, he made his own clothes from tree bark or animal skins.

As civilisation develops, people specialise in their respective activities. Those who manufacture products are different from those who cultivate crops. Within factories, one person concentrates on a small stage of the manufacturing process, another person on another stage. The final product is not the work of one person, but of many labourers. This division of labour makes it possible for each worker to become dexterous at the task he performs. It is this division of labour that facilitated inventions such as those for weaving, spinning and dyeing.

The extent to which you can specialise and divide your labour will be governed by the availability of markets. It is of no use specialising in the production of one product to the exclusion of others unless you can exchange it for the products of other people. You may specialise in catching fish knowing that you can sell them for money and use the money to buy the food and clothes you need. The market then is a necessary component of division of labour. If through division of labour you produce a lot but nobody buys a small portion of it, then you suffer losses and soon you will be out of business. Tobacco growers in Malawi know this situation too well.

Economic growth takes place where capital accumulates, says Smith. Capital accumulates through productive labour and not through unproductive labour. He differentiates productive labour from unproductive labour thus: "There is one sort of labour which adds to the value of the subject upon which it is bestowed: There is another which has no effect. The former as it produces a value may be called productive, the latter unproductive. Thus the labour of a manufacturer adds, generally, to the value of the materials which he works upon, that of his own maintenance and of his master's profits. The labour of a menial servant, to the contrary, adds the value of nothing. A man grows rich by employing a multitude of manufacturers; he grows poor by maintaining a multitude of menial servants." He went on to classify as unproductive the labour of the sovereigns, churchmen, lawyers, physicians, playwrights, buffoons, opera singers and so forth.

Smith calls productive labour that activity which at the end of the day leaves something tangible and valuable, not just emotional satisfaction. If you employ 20 persons to build a house and when they have done the job, there is a house to sleep in, to rent out or to sell, this is productive labour. If you hire 20 musicians and buffoons to entertain your guests at a wedding, it is a thrilling occasion indeed. You pay the entertainers but at the end of the day, they leave behind no product of permanent value which you can sell or which can continue to give you satisfaction.

Smith's concept of productive and unproductive labour is nowadays rejected. The GDP includes the value of both tangible products and services. It is recognised that in the absence of policemen and soldiers, no long-lasting industrial activity can take place because either internal brigands or foreign invaders will come and take away the products. Without the contributions of doctors and nurses in keeping the nation healthy, there cannot be much industrial and agricultural activity. Where there is poor health, there will be poor productivity resulting in low production.

There are certain activities which are extremely useful, but they do not assist directly in finding the things that feed the nation or those which we can sell. If you spend a million kwacha buying fertilisers and distributing them among farmers, at the end of the rainy season the nation might realise a bigger harvest than before. You could sell the surplus and earn the foreign exchange which might stabilise the kwacha. At the end of it, there might be less inflation in the economy.

But spend the same amount in court squabbling over who won the presidential election or whether the Senate should be reinstated; whatever the verdict, it won't contribute to the GDP. There will be no tangible and valuable product in place. This is what Smith had in mind when he spoke of unproductive labour. Those responsible for spending public funds should not ignore completely Smith's idea of productive and unproductive labour.

16 March 2001

THE PLIGHT OF MALAWIAN DESCENDANTS IN ZIMBABWE

When, less than two years ago, we learned that veterans of the Zimbabwean War of Independence were harassing white farmers and seizing their land, I expressed fears in this paper that people of Malawian origin might also be in trouble there. What I did not know then was that they could be as many as two million in number.

Their plight, as reported in the *Malawi News* of 10–16 March 2001, could hang over Malawi's head like the Sword of Damocles. The trouble is that most Malawians who are now in the public limelight are hardly interested in problems of Malawians of the Diaspora. Possibly they will start worrying about such people when they return home in an exodus even as the Arabs of Palestine started worrying when their fellow descendants of Abraham started arriving in droves at the end of the World War II to claim part of their ancestral lands.

Most Malawians were not yet born when a labour-recruiting organisation called *Mthandizi* used to send its agents all over Malawi enticing able-bodied men to emigrate to Southern Rhodesia and work on the farms. Those were the days of a booming economy for Zimbabwe. Farmers and miners were competing with those of South Africa for the hard-working, intelligent and rather docile Nyasa workers.

Most of those who were under the *Mthandizi* scheme were not accompanied by their wives. Many of them were unmarried. If those thousands, who in pre-independence days were reckoned at 200 000, have indeed multiplied to two million, they must have done so through their local wives. It is educated Malawians who went there as teachers, clerks and medical orderlies that usually sent for their wives. And these were fewer in number than labourers.

British newspapers and politicians have put up a hostile campaign against President Robert Mugabe. They wish he were replaced by someone who could stand up against the war veterans, some of whom seem to be trigger-happy. Malawi cannot afford to quarrel with Mugabe. We just have to talk with him and his henchmen in diplomatic language.

We have to let him know that when *Mthandizi* was recruiting labourers here, this country had a population of 2.5 to 4 million. Most of those who bear Malawian names there, like Phiri, Nyirenda and Khumbanyiwa are descendants of Malawians just as the Browns and Bushes of America are descendants of English people who migrated there centuries ago. They are now Americans.

Similarly, those people who went there under *Mthandizi* are now Zimbabweans. Many of them indeed have Zimbabwean mothers. Some of them may be third generation Zimbabweans. In the course of trying to resettle the Freedom War Veterans, displaced farm labourers have a right to be resettled within that country. To try to force them back to Malawi is to commit a very inhuman act.

In Malawi, land was owned on a communal basis. There were no freehold titles to it. You cultivated a piece of land which the village headman or chief allocated to you. If you went away and stayed there for years, the land was claimed by or allocated to other villagers. On return as *mtchona* (one who went away and stayed too long) you had no right to evict the persons you found cultivating the land you once cultivated.

This is indeed the most vexing part of the matter. Malawi's secondary industry economy is minuscule compared with that of Zimbabwe's. It cannot offer jobs to the returning *matchonas* or their descendants. They will find no free land waiting for them in the now highly congested rural areas of Malawi.

If SADC is to fulfil its role of ensuring economic and political cooperation between members, it must not sit silent when one country is trying to solve its labour and population problems with beggar-my-neighbour tactics. We must work in consultation. Malawi can perhaps absorb back a trickle of ethnic Maravi, but certainly not anything like one million, let alone two million. Zimbabwe will not be absorbing immigrants there for the first time. The Ndebele arrived in southern Zimbabwe only 50 years before the whites, as Ian Smith likes to inform the world.

Perhaps it is not realised that we Malawians are part Shona/Karanga in descent. Go to Mzimba and meet the Soko, Shonga, Matimba, Shumba, Shaba, Ndoro, Gumbo, Moyo and so on. You may say that this came about as a result of what was happening in pre-colonial days. But the fact remains that all of us, no matter where we are, were once strangers in the land we call ours.

When the British were occupying this country, they found local workers more interested in trekking southwards than working on local tea and coffee farms. These Europeans welcomed the arrival of the people they called Anguru but whom we know better as Lomwe from Mozambique. The survival and growth of tobacco, tea and coffee farms in Malawi was due to migrant Lomwe workers. They are the same Lomwe workers who built the Shire Highlands Railways, later called the Malawi Railways.

The Lomwes who came under this arrangement stayed permanently in Malawi. We do not regard them as Mozambicans anymore. Neither would it make any sense to remove any of such people from their gardens because 100 years ago that patch of land was occupied by members of another tribe.

Meanwhile, you people who claim to be leaders, spare a thought for problems like this instead of tiring the country with your power hungry politics.

HISTORY AS LITERATURE

When I was in the Civil Service holding a senior administrative position, I was surprised to find that one of the new recruits to be placed under me was a young Chancellor College graduate in physics, chemistry and biology. I asked him why he was there doing general administrative duties instead of being where he could apply his scientific knowledge. His reply was that his real aim when going to university was to prepare himself for an administrative career. "I did not want to study an arts or social science degree which might be more relevant to administration. You know I am one of those who are too lazy to study. To master history or English language books would have involved me in long hours of swotting."

This was quite revealing to me. So there are people who find it easy to solve a mathematical problem, penetrate the laws of physics but find history a bore. Yet these same people may be found enjoying poetry, music and reading a magazine with zest; why should they not enjoy a history book?

Bertrand Russell (1872–1970), British philosopher and mathematician, loved reading history. His reason: history is a desirable part of everybody's mental furniture in the same kind of way as is generally recognised in the case of poetry. If history is to fulfil this function, it can only do so by appealing to those who are not professional historians. I have myself always found very great interest in the reading of history.

If history is to appeal to non-historians, it must be written like literature, like a novel, and there should be elements of poetry in it. Yet it must not be forgotten that history is also a science subject. The writer of history must be scrupulous with facts. Happy is the writer who can write as an artist and yet be scientifically accurate.

Many budding writers in Africa suffer from the 'Me-also' disease. If someone writes a short love story, they also want to do the same; if someone writes a poem without rhyme or rhythm but which reads more like prose, they also do so. They are reluctant to go off the beaten track and attempt serious subjects like history, biography and biology which can be made delightful if written like literature.

Has anyone succeeded in doing this? Yes, from the time of the Greek historian Herodotus to date there have been historians who have combined art and science in writing their history. The result has been that their books have competed with novels in popularity and in enduring the ages.

One of such historians is Edward Gibbon (1737–94), the author of the classic *The Decline and Fall of the Roman Empire*. Gibbon's narrative is superb; his choice of words always masterly. His history is interesting because events are illuminated with the portraits of the men and women behind or responsible for those events.

Many history books are dull, especially those written simply to fulfil school syllabuses and requirements. These books dwell simply on events and do not portray the characters of those people who brought about those events. And so you read at length about the causes of the First and Second World Wars or what was the Federation of Rhodesia and Nyasaland. Men and women at the centre of such events are mentioned just in passing. Yet history is, as Thomas Carlyle puts it, "a biography of a country's heroes; suppress these in your narrative and you make the history unenjoyable".

As a sample of Gibbon, we may quote his portrait of Julian, one of the emperors during the decline and fall of the Roman Empire. "A more accurate view of the character and conduct of Julian will remove this favourable prepossession for a prince who did not escape the general contagion of the time... The actions of Julian are faithfully related by a judicious and candid historian... a devout and sincere attachment for the gods of Athens and Rome constituted the ruling passion of Julian."

In this, Gibbon fulfils what Russell regards as an ideal writer of history. He is interesting as an historian because in this narrative he has heroes and villains. Any attempt to be impartial when portraying the main characters of history will just make the book dull. What you should avoid is falsification of facts. There is nothing wrong with showing that you prefer Churchill to Hitler or vice-versa, provided your historical facts are accurate. Have a point of view.

A would-be writer of an interesting history book should first soak himself entirely in the facts. He should then get on with writing without now and again having to check up the facts. Checking of the facts should be done once the whole manuscript is completed. He should write with the fluency of an inspired novelist.

Thomas Babington Macaulay (1800–59), lawyer and historian, decided to write the history of England in a style that would be as interesting as that of a novel. Indeed he vowed his book would compete with the best novels in popularity. The publication of his *History of England from the Accession of James the Second* was a great event. His publishers, Longmans, are said to have paid him an advance of 20 000 pounds sterling. Try to convert the value of a 19th-century pound to a kwacha of today and you have someone who has made millions out of one well-written history book.

The collection of material may be done by a number of assistants or collaborators but the drafting of the book should be done by one person with a style that is engrossing to the general reader. This is how H.G. Wells wrote the great book *The Outline of History*. And this is how Winston Churchill wrote his great books on World War II which earned him the Nobel Prize for Literature, a rare recognition for an historian.

If the chapters of the book are written by different people, the book will lose fluency. That a book can be scientific (factual), historical and literary was proved by the publication of G.M. Trevelyan's *History of England* and *English Social History* before and during World War II, respectively. One of those who read the *History of England* page by page was Princess Elizabeth, later to become Her Majesty Queen Elizabeth II.

Writers with good style have made it possible for the general reader to enjoy and understand esoteric subjects like economics, astronomy and biology. While the contents of a book constitute the basics, the question whether it will be read widely depends on the style in which it is written.

Many people without a grounding in law would not wish to engage in disputations on legal or judicial questions; many outside the medical profession would just trust the advice of doctors on matters of health. But almost everyone who can read and write feels competent to comment on public or political affairs even though he has spent a lifetime in some other profession. People with such inclinations should take the trouble to read history. Things that happen today are partly influenced by what happened sometime back, and what is happening today will have an impact tomorrow. Whoever comments on public affairs when his knowledge of history is next to nil is most likely to air misleading views. But for non-historians to be interested in history, it is up to the professional historians to get away from the 'thesis style' of writing and to try to write like Gibbon, Macaulay, Voltaire and others. Write to be read.

3 December 2001

MALAWI'S IMMEDIATE ECONOMIC FUTURE

From newspapers we have learned that in the SADC region Mozambique's economy is the fastest growing. Some newspapers say that this year, despite the floods, the Mozambique GDP has grown by 15 per cent, whereas other SADC member countries have grown by less than five per cent.

On the face of it, this is puzzling. How is it that a country that has known anti-colonialism and civil wars for nearly three decades has managed to move faster than those countries which have enjoyed relative peace all this time? Mozambique's achievement is not unique, however. Once President Yoweri Museveni took charge of Uganda, world newspapers were similarly raving about his country as growing faster than any other in Africa.

Beyond Africa, and in an earlier period, we have the miracle achievements of Germany and Japan. These countries which had fought as allies in World War II, had their physical infrastructure heavily bombed. A good deal of their flowering youth had been killed. But by the mid-1960s Germany had emerged the richest country in Europe and still is. By the 1970s or 1980s, Japan was dominating world export markets and is now the second largest economy in the world while Germany is the third largest.

The outstanding economic growth of these countries may be explained both in terms of economic theory and social psychology. There was much American investment both in Germany and Japan. People there had a culture of hard work. They made up their minds that they were not going to waste their time on the misfortunes of the past, but were going to create new fortunes. Despite the losses occasioned by war, there still was a remnant of educated and skilled workers and entrepreneurs ready to seize economic opportunities.

Uganda had been known as the pearl of Africa. During colonial days, the Ugandans, especially the Baganda, prospered from the coffee industry. In East and Central Africa, they were the best educated. They had a university college called Makerere which was the destiny of degree-seeking students from surrounding countries. With the restoration of peace and political stability, there was a social and physical infrastructure on which to build the new economy.

Uganda received grants and other forms of aid from the European Union, World Bank and IMF, the USA and individual European countries.

Mozambique was not counted among the most developed of the African countries. Indeed, according to some accounts, it was one of the poorest countries of the World. With the end of the civil war, it is reported that there has been a good deal of direct investment into Mozambique, thanks to that government's progressive attitudes towards foreign investors. Some years ago, it was reported that the Mozambique government had invited South African whites to open farms in the Niasa (Nyasa) region. Recently the same government has invited Zimbabwean white farmers to resettle and farm in Mozambique. With such friendly policies towards foreigners, it is no wonder that direct investment is taking place on a sizeable scale in that country.

From what is happening in other countries, both near and far, Malawi must learn lessons. The fast development of the Mozambique economy offers opportunities for trade. We may buy from them and we may sell to them. You can do business only with a growing economy. However, since Mozambique's agricultural resources resemble ours, it is undoubtedly a competitor as well. Since Mozambicans are nearer the sea than we are, it is possible they are procuring their capital goods, including fertilisers, at less cost than we are. So we must examine our own costs and see where we can minimise them.

Malawi is not just in competition with other developing countries whose mainstay is agriculture. She is in competition with developed countries as well. Both North America and Europe are self-sufficient in farm products. The American management guru, Dr Peter Drucker, writes in *The Economist* of 3 November 2001: "For every one per cent by which agricultural prices and employment have fallen in the 20th century, agricultural subsidies and protection in every single developed country including America, have gone up by at least one per cent, often more. Protectionism in manufacturing is already in evidence although it tends to take the form of subsidies instead of traditional tariffs."

We must give top attention to the agricultural sector of the economy for three reasons. First, because it is the source of food. It should be our permanent policy to make the country self-sufficient in food because imported maize costs us too much, and deprives the country of the foreign reserves which could be better spent procuring drugs, fertilisers and capital equipment. Self-sufficiency in food does not or should not just mean self-sufficiency in maize. As President Bakili Muluzi has recently said, we Malawians should get used to eating other types of foods, instead of maize *nsima*. After all, people in lake shore districts like Nkhata Bay have for generations eaten their *nsima* made out of cassava flour. We should experiment with sweet potatoes, pumpkins and rice as full dishes instead of eating them as mere snacks.

Secondly, we must take care of agriculture so that we can export the surplus. Appeals have been made to developed countries to open their markets for agricultural commodities from developing countries. Rich countries are very reluctant to do so. An individual developing country of Malawi's size cannot succeed in persuading these large industrial countries to open their markets. It is here that economic groupings like SADC and COMESA could exert some kind of pressure.

Thirdly, agriculture must be developed as a source of raw materials for our own manufacturing industries. Our economic policy should aim at diversified agriculture instead of just relying on tobacco and tea for our cash crops. New cash crops should be tried; instead of just relying on maize for our food, other types should be tried too. Diversified agriculture should be supported by the diversified economy: manufacturing, tourism, etc.

This is the age of 'knowledge' industries. The wealthiest nations in the world are also the best educated. We must encourage our young people both at home and abroad to acquire technical and vocational knowledge that we can use in agriculture and secondary industries to compete with the rest of the world. We will benefit from the AGOA initiative only if we can display before the American buyer products that in price and quality are at least comparable with those from our competitors. Americans will not buy our products as a matter of goodwill to help us out of poverty. We are exposed to stiff competition; we must have the knowledge and technology that others have. Only then can we compete.

28 December 2001

WHO WILL PROVIDE THE ALTERNATIVE TO TOBACCO

That most people in Malawi are aware of the D-Day when the anti-smoking lobby will make the final onslaught on our tobacco industry, there is no denying. That there is an urgent need to diversify both the agricultural sector and the economy as a whole perhaps most people also know.

In *Nation Business Review* of 13 December 2001 an official of the National Economic Council (Nec) is quoted as saying: "The question (which must be asked and answered) is, why has Malawi not successfully diversified its production base yet? What are the stumbling blocks and what is the way forward?"

If the Nec does not have the answers to this question, then who could know better? Members of the public expect Nec to have data not only on the Malawi economy but also on the economies of those countries which could be our role models, like Japan, the Tigers of the East (Taiwan, South Korea, Thailand) and nearer home, Mauritius.

Whenever we seem to be at a loss, let us turn to the advice given by Dr Samuel Johnson, one of England's most brilliant men of the 18th century. He said, "Knowledge is of two kinds. We know a subject ourselves, or we know where we can find information."

We have heard of how Japan, after the Meiji Restoration in the 19th century, set about to imitate the technology of the west and to penetrate world markets. We have heard of the more recent industrialisation of countries of the Pacific Rim. There are books and journals aplenty on these countries, some of which ought to be stocked by Nec and scanned.

The current world economic philosophy seems to tally with Keynes about the role of the State in an economy, namely that the government should not do things which individuals are already doing, but it should do only those things which at present are not done at all.

Since what individual entrepreneurs do in one country does not correspond completely with what they do in other countries, we should expect the role of the State in the market economy to differ somewhat. Indeed, the welfare systems of European countries are more paternalistic than those of the United States, just to give one example.

This means that while Malawi must, in principle, embrace the ideals of the market economy, she must assign to its government a role in the economy that takes into account whether there are enough entrepreneurs and private resources in the country. Japan may have a lesson or two to teach us.

In a book of essays titled *Inside the Japanese System* and in an essay titled *The Way of the Bureaucrat*, Suzuta Atsuyuki says, "it was the Ministry of Finance bureaucracy that laid the foundations for the rapid growth of the economy and the doubling of Japan's national income, just as it was the Ministry of International Trade and Industry (MITI) bureaucracy that rehabilitated Japanese industry from the devastating aftermath of the war, directed the nation's productive energies into heavy industry, and stimulated industry to enhance its international competitiveness."

Indeed that bureaucracy well deserves its accolades for having turned Japan into the second largest economic force in the free world so quickly. At the height of its success, the élite walked tall and they might well have been likened to lions and tigers.

The picture drawn here about the role of the civil service is not that of 'hands-off' the economy. Rather the civil service in Japan took upon itself the roles of philosopher, guide and friend to private industry.

Atsuyuki goes on to tell us that recruitment to the civil service was very rigid; those who had come out with the best degrees from university were brought to the Ministry of Finance and MITI. New recruits were infected with the ethics of hard work and the devotion to one's master. True devotion was defined as the ability to endure. During the time the budget was being drawn up from September to December, the recruits were told to forget about Sundays and holidays and to just get on with the task in hand. Most civil servants worked as many as 200 hours overtime during such periods. Marriages had to be arranged for some of the young men who were too busy to go dating.

What we learn here is that the Japanese have paid special attention to staffing the civil service. We ourselves should constantly monitor the motivation, morale and performance of the civil service. Only first-class persons in every respect should be recruited to key ministries and jobs. Those civil servants who first work hard and then ask for better pay should have their pleas sympathetically considered; those who say give me better pay first before I work harder are a different case.

Who should diversify the Malawi economy? Both the State and the private entrepreneurs. The State should look at potential industries which private capital is reluctant to develop. The State has done this in the past. There is no reason why it should not do so again. I recall how the Chikangawa plantations started. I visited the area more than once when the government of the time started the plantation; the place was desolate. No private entrepreneur could think of starting those plantations which might not start yielding commercial products until a quarter of a century later. Private business people are after profits and dividends in the immediate future. Having laid down the foundations, the government has since sold the assets to private initiative.

With the proceeds from the privatised industries, the State should embark on diversifying the economy. At a later date these industries can be sold to private operators.

Identifying industries with potential may itself be difficult. But somewhere east or west, there are people with the knowledge, and whom we can consult for a fee. If Malawi is to diversify before it is too late, there should be enhanced willpower and ability. If we do nothing, nothing will happen.

<u>8 February 2002</u>

DEVELOPMENT
AND NATIONAL HONOUR

Why do countries like Malawi go hat in hand to seek development and financial assistance from rich and developed countries? They do so for several reasons.

To develop a country these days requires the use of advanced equipment and technology. To build a railroad, for example, you must have the machines such as are not already available in this country. You want the most modern medical hospital, go for the most modern equipment and drugs.

A country's ability to import goods it does not have depends on its export earnings. Unfortunately, export earnings of most underdeveloped countries fall short of their import requirements. These countries then approach the richer countries either to lend or grant them the wherewithal to procure the desired imports.

Developing countries also seek aid of the technical type. They may not have men and women of their own to man a hospital, a factory or to train staff. Therefore, they ask the developed countries for assistance in the form of personnel. Such people are usually referred to as technical advisors. They may assist as economists, constitutional lawyers, professors or planners.

Many of the rich countries of today did receive assistance from other countries that had undergone industrial transformation earlier. England was the first country to build railways. Other countries in Europe and the New World got technical and capital aid from her.

By approaching wealthy countries of today for developmental and budgetary assistance, underdeveloped countries are not necessarily being childish or parasitic. Of course those who receive and benefit from donors' assistance ought to be grateful. But in what form should their gratitude be?

Once upon a time, I knew a man who, by the standards of those days, had done well as a civil servant. He reached the position of senior executive officer, though his official title was Assistant District Commissioner. During colonial days for an African this was no mean achievement.

Whenever he visited his home on leave he took with him bands of bank notes and distributed them generously among his relatives, close and not so close.

He never forgot to tell people of neighbouring villages how he was shouldering the burden of clothing and feeding the whole of his village. He would ask someone "did you see how well dressed John and his wife turned up on Sunday? It is I who gave them those clothes. You see God has blessed me, I am rich. But you people are poor. The Devil has cursed you."

When his relatives heard of how he was exposing them to ridicule they just grinned. Sometimes they whined, "How humiliating it is to be poor. Wherever our brother goes he talks of nothing else but of how we owe everything we have to his wealth and open-handedness. But how did he get that good government job? His father sent him to school. Fine, we will also send our children to school."

Twenty or so years later, the children of these people had actually done better in school and obtained better jobs than the children of the well-to-do and boastful man. Then misfortunes came on him in a variety of forms. He became very poor. These other people now began laughing at him loudly. "Did you think we could not become well-to-do ourselves. Shame. The world is a transformer. See where he goes. Is that the man who used to sneer at our poverty, and throw bones to us instead of steak as if we were dogs?"

Some of the people who spoke like this had actually been assisted generously by that man. But because he had rendered his generosity in a condescending manner, the recipients of his gifts could not, deep in their hearts, feel real gratitude.

At the beginning of the African independence era, around about 1960, one often heard the phrase, "development aid without strings attached". That was the height of the Cold War, i.e. the rivalry between Western democracies and the Communist bloc. The developing countries were saying they wanted to receive assistance from either the east or the west without being obliged to embrace the ideology of either of the blocs.

Few of the African countries managed to retain such neutrality and yet receive the assistance. In those days, the western bloc did not insist on 'good governance' as a condition for granting aid. One-man dictatorships readily got aid provided they resisted any form of contact with the communists.

In fact, there has never been aid without strings attached. Developing countries have grumbled only when the strings have been too tight. Today, donors insist on good governance as a pre-condition for aid. A developing country applying for aid must adopt multiparty politics, the free press, poverty alleviation and so on. Only an evil-minded politician would, in principle, reject such conditions. But sometimes the term 'good governance' is too narrowly defined to mean govern your country as we govern ours. Such a pre-condition smacks of neo-colonialism.

No two democracies in the world are the same. The democracy practised in America is not the same as that in Britain, France, Germany or Japan. Until about two decades ago, women had no vote in Switzerland and yet nobody accused the Swiss of being undemocratic.

Just before gaining independence for Malawi, Dr Hastings K. Banda said he was going to make Malawi the Denmark of Africa, an aspiration that the Danes heard about with delight. It was a compliment for a country at the tip of the African continent to try to emulate them.

Round about 1965–66, I accompanied the then Minister of Finance to Copenhagen to negotiate for a Danish brewery to be located in Malawi. The Danish Government readily persuaded Carlsberg to come to Malawi. Thereafter, Malawi has been receiving aid from Denmark regularly.

But suddenly we hear Denmark will stop assisting Malawi for reasons none of which seem crucial. Most citizens of this country would be grateful if the person alleged to have misused Danish aid could be punished.

No country has succeeded in ridding itself of corruption completely. About three or four years ago, the whole Commission of the European Union was forced to resign when it was discovered it had engaged in corrupt practices. A senior British Minister had to resign last year for alleged corrupt dealings with an Indian business tycoon. A former German Chancellor, a French senior statesman and an Italian tycoon have had their names linked with shady dealings.

We are grateful to the Danes for the aid they have been giving us all these years. But they must not, through aid, try to compel us to handle affairs here exactly as they handle theirs. Let us hope the fair-minded Danes (and they are many) will persuade their government not to deprive the poor people of Malawi of the much-prized Danish aid.

2 April 2002

MANURE MAKING CAMPAIGN

I was in a Lilongwe hotel reading, once more, Pearl Buck's Nobel Prize-winning novel *The Good Earth*. I came to that chapter where the hero of the book, Wang Lung, declines his wife's suggestion that they sell one of their children into slavery in order to avert the child's and their own starvation.

I switched on the BBC TV documentary programme whose main theme I thought was Zimbabwe's wounded economy, but it featured Malawi as well.

My eyes came face to face with emaciated Malawians, among them a mother and her dying child. Has famine in Malawi indeed brought some people to such extremities? Now I understand better why President Bakili Muluzi has declared the country to be in a disastrous situation.

Just before noon I joined the staff of *The Nation* who were travelling to Chidzuma Village, T.A. Mkukula in Dowa District, to witness the launching of the manure-making campaign by the President.

As the road wound up the plateau of valleys and hills, we saw by the roadside square-shaped mounds of compost manure. Higher up on the hanging gardens were thickets of blossoming crops, realised through the use of organic manure.

In his curtain-raising speech, the Minister of Agriculture and Irrigation recited a modified version of the anecdote Booker T. Washington gave at the Atlanta Exposition in 1895 entitled 'Cast your bucket where you are'. The Minister spoke of a ship's captain that was pleading for fresh water from another ship thinking he was on the Indian Ocean when in fact he was at the mouth of the River Zambezi with its fresh water below and around his ship.

The moral of the anecdote was that people should know that the sources of soil fertility are right there in their backyards. There is a lot of outcry today about the shortage or expensiveness of fertilisers. There is pleading for subsidising of the fertilisers sold to farmers.

While it would be a benevolent gesture on the part of the Government to resume selling the fertilisers at give-away prices, we must not forget the opportunity costs. As you spend more and more public funds on fertiliser you have less and less money for subsidising university colleges which are thus compelled to reopen at irregular dates. The potholes in the roads must remain unrepaired when you divert funds to fertilisers. You reduce funds for drugs in the hospitals. The needs are numerous, the means to satisfy the needs are limited.

When confronted with such dilemmas, what we should do is to find out if higher crop yields can be achieved without using fertilisers. This is how the government, through the Ministry of Agriculture and Irrigation conceived the idea of mounting a manure-making campaign. Can manure feed crops as well as fertilisers? Yes: examples are there to see in Dowa and elsewhere in the country.

At the Chidzuma Village rally one of the distinguished guests was Dr G. Hannock Chinkhuntha. The name Chinkhuntha suggests a gigantic, bull-wrestling personality. But the Chinkhuntha I spoke to that day was a slightly built, soft-spoken gentleman who, over a period of about 20 years, has demonstrated beyond doubt that a good crop can be obtained from organic manure. Because you are unable to buy the expensive fertiliser it does not mean you are at your wits' end. There are several routes to the land of milk and honey. If a short and direct one is expensive why not take a longer but easily affordable one?

A healthy agricultural sector is cherished even in highly industrialised countries. The people of Europe have long realised that if you are totally dependent on other countries for your basic necessities, you could be easily starved to death during war times. Therefore, they take positive measures to have as much food grown at home as they can.

People who are always short of food will be too hungry to engage in the pursuits of science, arts and technology. While necessity is the mother of invention, a person with an empty stomach cannot think of anything else but food.

The benefits of organic manure were known by our forefathers before our British teachers introduced the teaching of agriculture in schools. In olden days our people practised shifting cultivation. Those were the days of plentiful land. After staying at one spot for a decade they would shift to another place. Often they planted crops on the ruins of the old village. In cattle-owning areas, the abandoned kraal produced a vigorous maize or tobacco crop. Seeds discarded into rubbish pits were known to sprawl into exceptionally good crops.

Resistance to change is the inclination that we must first overcome. Having been accustomed to the application of inorganic or chemical fertilisers there are some people who will not easily heed the advice 'cast your bucket where you are'. Whoever uses his tongue or pen during the manure-making campaign to encourage people into adopting compost manure will be doing the country a lot of good.

Whoever uses his tongue or pen to discourage farmers from heeding agriculture extension officers is doing the same harm to the wealth of Malawi as the one who harms the health of the nation by dissuading people from heeding programmes on HIV/Aids prevention. Sceptics think they are smarter than scientists. Often they are just plain ignorant. Without trying new ideas no nation can progress.

Diversification is a promising strategy against the onset of nationwide famine. This diversification must start at the production level. The adoption of organic manure does not mean the outright abandonment of chemical fertiliser. Both means of enriching the soil may be resorted to depending on the costs and benefits. There may be a lot of sweating involved in manure making, but remember at the end of the rain season all the bumper harvest belongs to the farmer. If he borrows money to buy fertilisers, not all the harvest will be his. The creditor will demand a portion.

THE KNOWLEDGE ECONOMY

Sometimes we lose our way in the struggle against poverty, ignorance and disease because we tend to ignore old truths. One of the common proverbs students of English learn in primary schools is 'knowledge is power'.

To the extent that there is knowledge in Africa, will Africa jettison the albatross around its neck which keeps it as the least developed and most miserable of the world's continents?

Africa is linked to the world economy at present as never before. The world economy is said to be a knowledge economy. Countries where knowledge is at a low level are lagging behind and getting poorer.

How do we acquire the appropriate knowledge? Dr Robert Laws, pioneer missionary of the Livingstonia Mission, used to quote a German proverb: "What you would like to have in the country, first put it in the schools." In other words, schools are the foundation of knowledge. An up-to-date educational system will generate wealth, other things being equal.

People erect schools for different purposes. For some, it is a means of catching the tender youth for their church or denomination. For others, education is business. For the State, schools must be established and reformed to cope with its development programme.

We talk a lot about poverty eradication or reduction. Who is to reduce or eradicate that poverty? The answer given is that the poor themselves will be empowered. Empowered with what? Perhaps we will give them free or subsidised fertilisers and access to low-cost credit. But as part and parcel of the global economy, we must adopt the priorities that the successful and wealthy countries of the world have adopted.

We must get away from the conception that agriculture alone can emancipate us from poverty. We have been growing cash crops like tea, tobacco and cotton for more than 100 years, but palpable prosperity continues to slip out of our hands. Time and time again, Africa in concert with other developing countries has appealed to developed countries to open up their markets to its exports, mostly primary products. The developed countries are unwilling to let in more than a fraction of these primary products unless they are trinkets of gold and diamonds.

As regards agricultural products, these countries insist on being self-sufficient and impose protectionist measures on imports.

The wealth of the world these days is generated through knowledge that enables countries to put into an economy information technology and other technologies. It is the tertiary industry for which the buying and consuming public seems to have an insatiable appetite.

The World Bank Institute's Journal for Fall (Autumn) 2001 titled *Development Outreach* is devoted to the knowledge economy. We are reminded there that throughout history the success of economies has been based on knowledge. The contribution of schools to knowledge and wealth is illustrated from Brazil, China and India.

Elements of the knowledge economy are visible in these very large developing economies. China has high-tech parks along its coast that 'are hotbeds of innovation'. Brazil is distinguished by world-class technological development in areas such as aeronautics, tropical agriculture and biotechnology. India has set up institutions doing research in agriculture, atomic electronics, environment, ocean, space, biotechnology, defence, health etc.

Though India and China are to Malawi what an elephant is to a mouse, they share with Malawi at least one common problem. This is too high a density of the population. How their agriculture manages to feed so many of their people is a matter of interest to us. The writer of an article on India says that India, having achieved the 'green revolution' which resulted in self-sufficiency in food, has gone on to achieve the 'white revolution' by producing more milk than any other country in the world.

Apparently, having discovered a formula for achieving self-sufficiency in food, Indians have never cast away that formula. They have continued not only to achieve self-sufficiency but even surpluses which they have exported. We achieved more than self-sufficiency under the Starter Pack Scheme but then slipped down from the summit and once more we have to make ends meet on charity. What did the Indians do to maintain the momentum?

China is interesting because of its flexible economic philosophies. In the minds of many outsiders, China is the last bastion of communism, inward-looking and scornful of capitalism. But in practice, China is no classic communist state.

In its publicly sponsored high-technology and science zones, foreign-owned enterprises now account for three quarters of the exports and labour productivity is twice as high as the rest of the economy.

We usually have the impression that in a socialist or communist country, the State meets the entire cost of educating citizens. But China is also tapping private resources: one-third of China's higher education costs are now borne by students, not the government, and four million students are presently studying at privately funded tertiary education institutions. The country is also developing international alliances in education. Beijing University alone has relationships with 100 universities.

There are two points here to relate to our own experience. When the Malawi Government announced that university students were going to make the bigger contributions to the cost of their education, students were indignant and made disturbing protests. Their parents and guardians tacitly supported these demonstrations in that they did little to calm down the tempers of their sons and daughters. But then see what students in a socialist country are doing.

Private participation in education in Malawi has been accorded a higher place with the advent of the multi-party era. But hostile attitudes are still hanging around. A diploma or certificate from a private school is viewed with prejudice.

The officials keep on telling holders of such certificates or diplomas that their school is not a public examiner and that they recognise certificates from public examiners only. Yet the private school may have issued its own diploma to the students precisely because there are no public examining bodies for that particular course in Malawi or abroad.

Educational systems in knowledge economies prepare their students for life-long learning. Experience alone cannot make individuals or countries hold their own in a knowledge economy because knowledge is constantly growing and changing.

In Malawi there is a great anxiety about standards of education. To be at par with world standards, Chinese educational institutions, as we have noted above, are linked to foreign institutions. How many linkages have our own educational institutions established? To cope in the knowledge economy, our schools must be comparable with nothing but the best in the world.

11 November 2002

THE PERENNIAL FOOD PROBLEM

F rench presidents have a lot to teach us about agricultural policies. When you know on which side your bread is buttered do not let your colleagues make you munch on the wrong side.

Mention the EU's Common Agricultural Policy (CAP) and you cannot help but think of the overarching interests of French farmers. Despite protests from presidents or prime ministers like Britain's Tony Blair, at a recent summit meeting of EU leaders in Brussels, President Chirac of France was able to persuade other delegates to retain the status quo of the CAP.

About half of the EU budget is spent on subsidising agriculture. Said Chirac: "We were able to agree a spending regime that will guarantee a dynamic EU agricultural sector that will be able to maintain its position as a major exporter in the years to come. I think this is a good deal for us."

So the most industrialised countries in the world have no intention of opening agricultural markets to non-industrialised countries like Malawi. The argument and the plea that the best way to help developing countries is to open the EU market to them, the presidents have heard time and time again, but they have their farmers to think about first. After all, their farmers vote in French general elections; farmers of the developing countries do not vote in French general elections.

In the *Daily Times* of 7 November 2002 we learn that a UK non-governmental organisation, the World Development Movement (WDM), has accused the twin organisations – the World Bank and International Monetary Fund (IMF) – of having imposed on Malawi Structural Adjustment Programmes (SAPs) which have resulted in stop-go food crises over the last 20 years.

Though it is not good for a country or individuals habitually to blame others for their failures and problems, sometimes it is correct to lay the blame where it should be. The World Bank and the IMF are friends of developing countries. Without them and their rescue operations possibly some developing countries would have invited their former colonial masters to come back. Their policies and recommendations seem to be well-meaning, but as the old saying goes, the road to hell is paved with good intentions. In Malawi as in most developing countries the IMF/World Bank structural adjustment programmes have yet to prove a great success.

In Malawi chronic inflation is attributed to government appetite for private sector loans. By borrowing from the public, the government is said to be forcing interest rates up and is crowding out private would-be borrowers and investors. As one Asian businessman told me: "I would rather invest my savings in Treasury Bills and earn a steady income than invest to make new products and be forced to sell them at high prices in order to meet my bank interest repayments."

When we talk of government borrowing we are likely to be critical. But we have to ask, what is the borrowed money used for? Once we know this we are in a better position to judge if the borrowing is unwise or not.

A family man who falls into debt in order to go on a holiday, watch football or buy a TV is one type of borrower; a family man who borrows money to buy food for his starving children or to pay private hospital bills is another.

Can we blame the government if it borrows money to meet the cost of providing free food to the needy and free farm inputs to those who cannot afford to buy their own. Must people be abandoned to starvation so that interest rates may continue to slide downwards? If government postpones supplying free inputs before the onset of the rains, is that the best way to ensure a bumper harvest next year?

One gets the impression from time to time that something is wrong both on the side of the granting and on the side of the aid-receiving bureaucracies. We learn quite often that the IMF/World Bank have withheld the funds they pledged because the Malawi government has failed to implement this or that programme. Whenever this allegation is valid, is it because of incompetence on the part of our civil service or just some kind of devious behaviour?

The policy of the individual donors to withhold their own pledge until IMF/World Bank are satisfied with what is going on in this country compounds our hardships. Why should individual donors who budgeted their aid package independently not proceed to release funds while the IMF/World Bank are sorting out their difficulties with the government of a developing country? Sometimes one feels that we are being cornered by the wealthy nations.

At the same time we need to review the performance of our civil service whenever the need arises. We say these days that governments cannot help being entrepreneurial. They have got to see that projects are launched, businesses are doing better and there is general economic development. When we say government in this case we mean the civil service more than the political segment. It is the civil service that has the technical experience, the planning machinery and the essential information.

If there are bureaucratic and technical weaknesses in the civil service, then of course there will always be problems in our relationships with donors. IMF and the World Bank pledges will continue to be withheld when they are needed most.

How would you feel when in London someone shows you a newspaper feature that says in Malawi famine has reduced people to eating mice? The writer says he saw this happen in Mchinji.

Those who write about this country's hunger problem should know that we expect sympathy to be obtained on the basis of facts. For many people in Malawi mice are as much a delicacy as prawns are in England. Here some people eat mice regardless of the state of food in the country.

9 December 2002

THE EFFECTS OF EMIGRATION

Emigration means leaving one's own country to settle in another. On departure from your country you become an emigrant while on arrival in the foreign country you become an immigrant.

One of the constantly debated issues these days is the emigration of highly educated and skilled Africans. Fifty years or so ago the few highly educated Africans of those days launched or joined campaigns for independence partly because they said their colonial rulers were excluding them from the best jobs.

Upon gaining independence, schemes were hatched to accelerate localisation of jobs, especially in the public service until eventually all the plum jobs were held by *Wanachi*, sons and daughters of the soil. The paradox now is that some of the best-educated Africans prefer to work abroad, especially in the rich countries of the United States, United Kingdom and continental Europe. They decide to remain there after completing their higher degrees even when their own countries need them back.

Why do people choose to emigrate? In the past, as in the present, emigration was engineered by a mixture of compulsion and volition. Circumstances – political and economic – have been behind recent emigrations. Every tribe in Malawi has a story about where its ancestors came from. Perpetual political instability and war in the Great Lakes Region forced ancestors of the Chewa, Tumbuka, Tonga and others to quit that belt of Africa.

Those that left, on arrival found other people settled here, intermarried with them and adopted new languages. Shaka's Mfecane drove out other Nguni and Sotho clans while the advent of Portuguese rule in northern Mozambique was a major factor of Lomwe emigration.

While some people have settled in one place for centuries others have preferred a nomadic life in search of greener pastures. Searching for better opportunities, for jobs and income is the major factor behind émigré Africans.

It is not only Africans who emigrate. Even between developed countries there is a good deal of migration. It is said many British and Canadian students in America remain there to pick up higher-paid jobs. The current of prosperity has a propensity to change direction. When the economy of one country is in a boom that of another is in recession – migration then takes place from the latter to the former.

An African student who had done very well in his overseas course was asked by his professor why he did not want to return to his country. He replied that he belonged to the wrong tribe and could not expect to be offered a job back home commensurate with his qualifications.

It is true that some highly qualified Africans had to stay away from their countries because of discrimination of sorts. How many Malawians have heard the name Dr Emily Maliwa? In the early 60s when she was a postgraduate student at the University of London, I joked with her and said: "Pleased to meet you again Miss Malawi" She said "hello" and then pondered over what I had said. "Oh yes, it is a matter of transposing the 'i' and 'a' and then Maliwa becomes Malawi."

There was a genuine compliment in my remark. In those days when very few Malawian women were abroad for study and those who were there were studying domestic science or nursing, here was a girl from Mulanje having taken a BA in India, an MA in the United States and who was now at one of the most prestigious universities in the world doing research for her PhD.

Back home, about the year 1966 or 1967, the first Malawian female PhD sought a job at the newly founded University of Malawi. Though there was a vacancy, on instruction from the top of the political hierarchy, the University Council refused to employ her. She migrated to Zambia and then to the United States. She returned to this country at the dawn of the multiparty era, about 1993. But she was in poor health and did not live much longer.

It is true then that some African intellectuals and scientists are abroad because they have been rejected by their countries. But for the majority it is the salary differential that has been the decisive factor.

Host countries usually welcome these highly qualified foreigners, even those from poor countries like Malawi. The enduring success of the United States in science and technology owes a good deal to guest or émigré personnel of high calibre. There are said to be one million Indians in the United States, most of them with university degrees. Thirty per cent of educated Ghanaians live and work abroad.

Even countries like Britain and Germany have placed fewer obstructions on the immigration of skilled people. It is recognised that in the present world knowledge is power as never before. A country that does not keep up with advances made in other countries will wake up one day to find itself laggard.

Does emigration benefit the country of departure as compared with the country of destination? The history of modern Malawi is that of a country whose citizens, both educated and uneducated, have been going out in thousands annually until about 20 years ago. How has this helped or hindered the growth of the Malawi economy?

During colonial days government could afford to tax Malawians lightly because the economy was benefiting from the remittances of Malawians working abroad, especially in Southern Rhodesia (Zimbabwe) and South Africa.

Though economically the Northern Region was lagging behind the other two regions, people there were not worse off in matters of dressing. Some such as those of Nkhata Bay pioneered in building good brick houses. This was largely due to the money brought home by people who had gone to work abroad. But employers in Malawi were often complaining that they were being deprived of the most able-bodied men. Many of those who went out never returned and this created hardships for mothers, wives and children.

Among present-day Malawian emigrants are doctors, nurses, engineers, university dons. If these people had to leave or remain abroad because the mother country did not offer them jobs commensurate with their qualifications we cannot blame them. In a state of unemployment or under-employment one cannot achieve much.

But we must keep on reminding them that the country has not been able to offer them good jobs because it is under-developed and poor. All Malawians both at home and abroad have a duty to contribute to the country's development. Those who have built up savings should buy shares in Malawian companies or Treasury Bills. In this way they will be injecting into the economy one of the factors of economic growth, namely capital. Those who have acquired rare skills should consider returning home before they are too old to work.

Some should choose to spend their sabbaticals in Malawi and take up temporary jobs or lectureships with the aim of sharing their knowledge and expertise with their compatriots.

ECONOMIC HARDSHIPS

Often as I trudge along the streets of Blantyre, someone stops me to check on my feelings about the current economic conditions. Times are hard, the economy is stagnant. No, it is getting worse. See, companies are closing and laying off their workers in droves.

This man says the President is not getting good advice. He has surrounded himself with many advisors, but some of them are only collecting, not earning their salaries. They are not really giving the President the right suggestions about solving this country's economic problems.

Most of my contacts lay the whole blame on the Government for the country's economic hardships. If only the President could get tough with the sharks in his Cabinet, they say, things would be better.

In times of widespread pestilence, accusations of witchcraft are easily believed. Sometimes accusations take a ferocious turn, as witnessed by the news from Mzimba, where a village headman and his people recently murdered a 60-year-old man on suspicion of being a wizard. Such accusations have been common in the tribal history of Malawi, but since the advent of British rule in 1891 the execution of suspects has been rare.

People sometimes reported suspicious deaths to the District Commissioner and pointed their fingers at someone. The District Commissioner would send a medical doctor, who would order the dead body to be exhumed. In most cases, the post-mortem revealed that the person had died of natural causes. People would then say: "Ah well, white people do not understand African witchcraft."

When discussing the current economic plight of the country, we should avoid being parochial or unduly pessimistic. Rather, we should do so in the context of globalisation. Perhaps some of our country's hardships stem from the fact that the world economy as a whole is sick.

The Economist issue of 28 September, 2002, featured *Doldrums: The world economy and how to rescue it.* Inside there is a survey of the world economy and particularly the American economy, which for more than a decade has been upwardly mobile, but is now in a state of recession. Japan has been in such a situation for 10 years. In both countries low interest and inflation rates are proving of little help for revival of the giant economies.

What we are witnessing now is the collapse of orthodox and revolutionary economic theories. The advent of the Industrial Revolution in Britain in the 18th and 19th centuries ushered in a phenomenon called the trade or business cycle. For about eight or ten years, an economy would be growing fast, jobs would be chasing after job seekers. Almost everyone in business would be making a tidy profit.

Then, about turn. Once a giant company hits the ceiling, profits tumble, workers are laid off. Those other companies that used to depend on it as a supplier and customer now cannot obtain the components they needed for their businesses, while others are no longer receiving orders for their products. What has started as the decline and death of one company now becomes the epidemic that threatens the whole economy.

Several explanations were given for this economic instability. A boom might take place following the discovery of minerals or oil. Growth based on these discoveries would come to an end once these assets had wasted away. A series of inventions might introduce into an economy new types of business, e.g. the invention of the railway system, the telegraph, the wireless and electricity. All these and more introduced into the economy new products, services and opportunities for employment.

After the greatest depression in capitalist history following the 1929 American stock market crash, John Maynard Keynes of Cambridge University issued his epoch-making book, *The General Theory of Employment Interest and Money*, in which he advocated government intervention in the economy to resuscitate or maintain demand. This intervention could take the form of public works; government would spend money building or repairing roads and bridges. In so doing, it would generate the money to be spent on consumer goods. Revival of demand in the economy would act as an inducement to business people to reopen old factories and start new ones.

The main tools for maintaining or reviving demand were fiscal and monetary. By fiscal we mean the level and type of taxes that a government adopts and the manner in which it spends the proceeds. By monetary policy we mean central bank policy regarding interest rate, liquidity in the economy and credit expansion or contraction.

After the end of World War II, Keynesianism held sway in most market economies, especially in Anglo-Saxon countries. Economies grew at steady rates. Some economists used to herald the Keynesian era as the death of the business cycle. They thought the alternation of boom and bust was a thing of the past.

But wait a minute. By the 1970s, major economies were experiencing recessions which were being aggravated by the oil price hikes following Arab-Israel wars.

A new economic phenomenon had risen in which inflation existed at the same time as general economic stagnation. The phenomenon was called stagflation. Some economists blamed it on government intervention in the economy.

Great and influential economists such as Milton Friedman of the United States advocated untrammelled private enterprise and minimum government participation in the economy. They talked and wrote as if private enterprise would provide all the solutions.

A new corps of economists is blaming the current slump on the behaviour of giant companies and their corrupt managers, who fiddle with accounts, do insider trading and lead the companies to bankruptcy while they themselves walk out with hefty terminal benefits. When the American Congress (parliament) asked Alan Greenspan, Governor of the Federal Reserve Bank, if fiscal and monetary policies acting at their optimum could eliminate business cycles he answered: "In my judgment, no, because there are no tools to change human nature. Too often people are prone to recurring bouts of optimism and pessimism."

What lessons are there for us in Malawi? The Government and the Reserve Bank may put forward the policies for the revival of the economy, but unless we respond with the right moods and activities, the day of economic recovery may be far away. Neither the Government nor the people have the power and resources to improve the economy overnight, but by working in partnership they can achieve a measure of success.

In plain language, at last God has sent us the rains. Government has distributed free seeds and inputs. If people put in extra effort, the country may realise a bigger harvest in 2003 and this could usher in the positive side of the business cycle.

THE COMMON IN MANKIND

The father of the Pan-African Congress, Dr W.E.B. DuBois, wrote at the beginning of the last century that the problem of the 20th century would be the colour question between the fair-skinned and the dark-skinned. He lived to the age of about 95 and died as a naturalised Ghanaian without seeing the end of apartheid.

Colour questions will not figure much during the 21st century. Rather it will be the culture war. The earth is becoming one country, one city but not one nation or one community. Colour has become less of a fascination, because in most countries children are born into multi-racial communities. They know from the start that, just as a dove is a dove regardless of colour, so a person is still a human being whatever his or her colour.

I remember during my childhood days that to see a white person was great news up north. When a government official or missionary pitched his tent in one village, people from surrounding villages flocked there to have a look at him. Thereafter, they would engage in discussions about him and the marvellous possessions he had with him such as the camera, the tea-things, the boots on his feet, the big mirrors and so on.

Those were the days before the politics of nationalism and federation came to the fore. People could be heard to say: "God has given these white people the intelligence to do everything except to conquer death."

While Africans thought white people could do anything, the average white person, even loving and kind ones, had a low view of what the African could do. In 1952, while Dr Hastings Kamuzu Banda was agitating against the proposed Federation of Rhodesia and Nyasaland he wrote in a journal published in London called *East Africa and Rhodesia*: "You [white people] grossly underestimate our intelligence."

He was responding to an editorial in which it was suggested that once Africans saw the economic benefits of the federation they would have nothing to do with politics.

I was told by the late S.F. Muwamba that an Afrikaner woman, when told that there was an African doctor wondered if he was a *Sangoma*, a herbalist, or a diviner. When told the man had medical degrees from British and American universities she was quite astonished. The only black people she had known were her farm boys and domestic servants. She had never imagined that black people could go beyond that.

What breaks prejudice is contact. In the last 50 years or so, thousands of Africans have been to the most renowned European and American universities. Some have held senior positions with distinction. After all, we have Kofi Annan holding the topmost international civil service job as Secretary General of the United Nations. The fact that he has been given a second term without dissent is evidence enough that he is doing well.

Culture is likely to be the source of conflict during the 21st century. Because of civil wars, or for economic reasons, people of many countries have migrated. Many of these find it difficult to give up their traditions. On 26 October 2002 I saw at Heathrow Airport one old woman drawing the attention of another to a man from the Indian sub-continent. The man was dressed in a style that may be impressive elsewhere. But to those women he looked something of a clown. It was not his brown colour that repelled them because right there people were being served by a person we would call Asian. It was the man's culture reflected in the style of his dress that made him strange in the eyes of those London women.

The differences that exist between people are man-made rather than natural. There is a good deal that naturally unites persons of one race with those of another. Even if we speak different languages we are able to learn each other's language. We have common sentiments of love, hatred, kindness, cruelty, laughter and weeping. These you find in humans everywhere and anywhere.

Tutors in fiction writing advise budding writers: you do not have to travel the world over to write a story or book that will appeal to people of many nations. Just observe and record faithfully the emotions of the people in your own village or town, for the human natures you find in your village are the same world-wide. It is only the environment that makes the difference.

On 23 October 2002 I was in a group of delegates from various African and other countries at a forum east of the Andes, in Ecuador. One man called Kongo was explaining how an irrigation scheme had been launched. People were scrambling to be close to him and to the interpreter.

I found myself crowded out. I went and stood on a rock a little distance away. Three 'African' girls approached me. One of them said something I could guess was friendly. I beckoned one of the Spanish speakers and asked her what the girl was saying.

"She says do you like what you see here?" she told me and I said I liked it very much and thanked her for having spoken to me.

"Why don't you also visit us in Africa?" I asked and they told me they were trying to make contacts.

There are people with positive approaches and there are people with negative approaches to human relations. The positive notice what unites mankind and wish to promote it, the negative see what separates and want to aggravate it.

Our duty is to encourage the facts of life on which we agree regardless of religion, race or nationality. Most people believe that peace is better than war. These people should cooperate in promoting peaceful coexistence between nations and jointly stand up against aggressive dictators and terrorists.

There is a lot of injustice within and between countries. The rule of law should prevail within nations and between nations. Those nations which disagree over anything such as boundaries should take their differences to the International Court of Justice in The Hague, Holland.

Our religious doctrines and practices need to be reviewed so that the manner in which we practise them does not result in quarrels and conflicts with people of other faiths. Some of the practices mentioned in the holy books were relevant to the places and times when the prophets first launched the religions. They are not part of eternal truths.

Take for example the canon law which says a woman who bears a child out of wedlock should be stoned to death. Is the woman condemned because of having slept with a man who was not her husband or simply because she has borne an illegitimate child. If the woman sins when she sleeps with a man who is not her husband then the authorities must execute all prostitutes. This might be a holy act, but not a humane one.

Our world has shrunk so much that it no longer makes sense to talk of Africa for Africans, Asia for the Asians, and Europe for the Europeans. The whole world has become a rainbow of nations. We must emphasise what binds us, not that which splits us.

REGIONAL AND TAIFA TRADERS

Recently there have appeared articles in our weekly and daily press about 'Taifa' traders at Mzuzu, meaning traders from Tanzania. The word taifa simply means 'nation' in the Swahili language. Most Malawians became familiar with the word after independence. Our national football team regularly played against Tanzania's national team, the Taifa Stars.

The news items indicated that the Tanzanian traders have been given a market of their own at Mzuzu by the City Assembly, and that they are very popular with buyers from all over the country. Women who usually flock southwards to make their purchases in Harare and Johannesburg now source their needs from no farther than Mzuzu.

As usual, when cheaper imports enter a trading centre, citizens' reactions are mixed. Those who buy to consume welcome the cheaper prices. Those who manufacture similar products view the cheaper goods as a threat to their own businesses. In such a situation the ministry responsible for trade or economic matters may take action, or no action, depending on whether or not it feels the interests of local producers are more important than those of local consumers.

Most Malawians are more conscious of economic links with southern Africa, especially Zimbabwe and South Africa. This is so because for decades Malawians were recruited in their thousands to work in the once-booming farms and mines south of the Zambezi. But our connections with the east coast have a longer history.

From history books we learn of the 'Warundi' (Lundu's people) and the 'Wazimba' people fighting their way up to Mombasa to protect their trade links from the Portuguese. This was in the dim 16th century. More clear are the traders from Zanzibar. Around 1840, Jumbe arrived at Nkhotakota. And in 1884 Mlozi, also from the east coast, arrived at Karonga.

These Arab/Swahili traders were not popular either with the local people or with the incoming British empire-builders. This was because they were not just interested in trade but also in political power. Jumbe succeeded in unseating at least two chiefs of Nkhotakota. Mlozi also talked of driving out Ngonde chiefs and of becoming sultan. Bloody feuds took place between Mlozi's men and Ngonde sub-chiefs such as Kasote and Mwenimtete.

What made the east coast traders even more unwelcome was the merchandise they were seeking. They had come to buy the ivory that commanded high prices in overseas markets. They also bought slaves to carry the ivory and later sold them in the Zanzibar slave market. To obtain slaves they armed local brigands or engaged in raids themselves to capture people from unarmed villages and tribes.

All attempts by the British traders and missionaries to persuade Mlozi to quit the land of the Ngonde failed. He found living and trading there very profitable. But after a skirmish with the protectorate forces, Mlozi was hanged in 1895. His band of traders vanished. Mandala stores took over. At about the same time, a successor of Jumbe at Nkhotakota was deported to Zanzibar.

How do we handle these modern-day east coast traders? Immigration authorities have hinted that the people trading at Mzuzu are without the necessary immigration documents. In the recent past we have read of the deportation of aliens including Nigerians, Pakistanis and Tanzanians; the last of these from the Northern Region, the region nearest to Tanzania.

While foreigners who enter the country must be subject to thorough immigration checks, the deportation of traders should be done hesitantly. We cannot be talking of the SADC and COMESA economic groupings and at the same time be hostile to those who want to do business here unless there is evidence that their trading activities injure our economy.

For a variety of reasons, merchandise in Tanzanian shops has always been cheaper than in Malawi. In the past many Malawian retail shopkeepers travelled to Tanzania, even as far as Dar es Salaam, to obtain stock. The journeys that Malawians now make to Zimbabwe and South Africa they were in the 1960s making to Tanzania. At this time I was living in Dar es Salaam and used to see Malawians buying merchandise that had been imported from the Indian subcontinent and the Middle East.

We are faced with a baffling situation. The text-book theory of international trade tells us that countries that specialise in making and selling goods in which they have a comparative advantage realise higher living standards by trading with one another. For Malawi, the trouble is that we and our neighbours seem to have the same products. The soils and climate which are favourable to the growing of tobacco, tea, coffee and sugar, are also found in neighbouring countries. What one country produces, another also produces. There is no natural comparative advantage in this situation. Thus instead of the traders of one country complementing those of another, they actually compete with them. Sometimes they engage in unorthodox tactics to undercut each other. The losers then appeal to their governments to create artificial trade barriers against the competing imports.

Taifa traders should be treated as welcome, not only because they are bringing into the country goods which Malawians would have to go to Johannesburg to buy but also because diversification in sourcing has advantages. To rely simply on Zimbabwe and South Africa as sources of our supply is not in the interest of our economy. See what has happened in Zimbabwe. The economy there has gone bad because of both political and natural causes. The depreciation of the Zim dollar has so cheapened Zimbabwean exports that they undercut our local products. This is welcome to the consumer, but not to the local Malawian manufacturer, who now faces bankruptcy, or to the local Malawian exporter whose products are now more expensive in the Zimbabwe market.

In regional trade no country can survive economically by simply practising the tenets of comparative advantage. Developing countries grow the same commodities and developed countries manufacture the same goods. Regional trading depends on "you buy from us and we will buy from you".

AFRICANS OF THE DIASPORA

The word Diaspora means dispersion. It has generally been used in reference to the dispersion of the Jews after the Babylonian and Roman conquests. Nowadays it is regularly in use with regard to Africans who, for historical or economic reasons, live in foreign countries. Some have been citizens of those countries for many generations, but they still identify themselves with the fortunes and misfortunes of their ancestral nation.

African-Americans have their roots in Africa. We have a duty to take an interest in their history, because it provides lessons that should not be forgotten. The ancestors of today's African-Americans were forcibly taken from their tribal homelands. They were unable to defend themselves against slave traders. They were also vulnerable to the avarice of fellow Africans, with their desire for the white man's beads, clothes, alcohol and guns.

Referring to Joseph, son of Jacob, Judah said: "What profit is it if we slay our brother and conceal his blood? Come let us sell him to the Ishmaelites." Most of the sons of Jacob hated their half-brother Joseph, their father's favourite. Besides, they regarded him as arrogant. When he followed them into the bush where they were tending their father's sheep, they decided to sell him into slavery.

Selling relatives in this treacherous manner was common in this country until the arrival of British rule. There was the practice of *chifwamba* (kidnapping), whereby some people would pounce on someone and then sell him to the Arabs/ Swahilis from the east coast of Africa, especially Zanzibar and Kilwa. In this way thousands of people from this corner of Africa found their way to other countries. Many were sold to the Portuguese, who took them to the Americas.

In October 2002, I had the good fortune to be part of a Food and Agricultural Organisation delegation to Ecuador. There I was much interested in talking to the Africans of the Diaspora that I met working on irrigation schemes. Very often when we talk of the descendants of Africa we have in mind those in the United States and the West Indies. Little do we realise that there are clusters of African descendants in several Latin-American countries also. Those I met in Ecuador struck me as having preserved their African-ness perhaps even more than the African-Americans and the West Indians. Though the majority of slaves were taken from West Africa, those I saw in both Ecuador and Guatemala could come here, walk among us and not be recognised until they started talking.

The history of the Diaspora started in the 15th century, when Portuguese navigators exploring the western side of Africa to find a route to India captured a few Africans, possibly in Congo or Angola, and took them home as slaves. They proved themselves good toilers. In South America, the Portuguese and Spanish were over-working the native Indians on their estates. These people were dying and their populations dwindling. A Spanish priest, Las Casas, proposed to the estate owners that they go to Africa and buy slaves. In this way began the trade in human beings.

In the Ecuadorian city of Quito, our guide took us into a Franciscan cathedral which in grandeur vies with Cologne Cathedral. In the past, he told us, those who went to Mass were grouped so that white men were seated nearest to the pulpit, after them white women, next sat the native Indian men and women and lastly, and farthest away, were the black people. Thus for ages, in any encounter with people of other races, the African was the underdog.

All the same, some Africans of the Diaspora achieved eminence. The grandfather of the great Russian writer Aleksander Pushkin was an African soldier in the Russian Army. The grandmother of the French author Alexandre Dumas, writer of *The Three Musketeers*, was an African slave.

Some Africans who were taken to the United States felt they had a duty to contribute to the emancipation of Africa. They founded churches and sent missionaries to Africa. They introduced a brand of teaching here known as Ethiopianism. They interpreted 'Truth shall make you free' to mean free from both sins and slavery or foreign domination. One of their strong adherents was John Chilembwe of Malawi.

The idea of African unity started in America with men such as W.E.B. DuBois and Marcus Aurelius Garvey. DuBois guided Pan-African congresses which supported post-World War II African leaders such as Kwame Nkrumah of Ghana, Jomo Kenyatta of Kenya and Hastings Kamuzu Banda of Malawi.

There is need for further research into the history of people of African origin scattered overseas.

DEVELOPMENT AND THE ENVIRONMENT

Recently I stopped at Mzimba Market to buy a type of fish called *nthuwi*, which in my boyhood days I had enjoyed hooking out of the River Rukuru. What the vendor offered me were such tiny fish that I had to remind him that the Government is appealing to fishermen not to trap specimens that are too young. "We do this because we have no other work to do," he said.

This is the kind of reply you would get if you tried to argue with someone who is depleting forests in the course of making charcoal for sale in town. He wants to clothe and feed his family today. The future will take care of itself as far as he is concerned. It is hard trying to convince people such as these that economic development that ignores the environment is doomed to vanish sooner rather than later.

Environmental degradation takes a variety of forms. River water may be polluted to the extent that even if you touch it you feel that you are already catching a disease. Most Sundays I take a walk to Ndirande Market and briefly stop on the bridge to look at the river flowing underneath. The water carries along all manner of debris; thrown-away pieces of cloth, broken gourds, leaves, twigs and nondescript matter. Most of the water is muddy; sunlight cannot pass through it.

Somewhere on both sides of the bridge you see children either washing clothes or bathing. They seem to find pleasure in wading through what looks like contaminated water. Filthy environments like this have given birth to a new disease in the Far East called Sars.

Concern for economic development and the economic environment are not alternatives, but Siamese twins. If you deal with one but ignore the other, you ultimately forfeit both. A common phrase in the art and science of today is 'sustainable development': the development that lasts for many generations, not just one.

Those who engage in the wanton cutting of forest trees for charcoal or plants to sell in town may think they are alleviating their poverty, and some may think they are making themselves rich. But this is just temporary. When all the trees are cut, heavy rains denude the land of its fertile soils. The land will be unable to support the next generation, a generation that will be bigger than that of today.

The best way to ensure that the income you earn today will still be available in the future is to avoid destruction of your resources. This will entail restraining your exploitation and consumption habits. Just as a person who saves part of his salary today will have some money to live on in later days, so a community that does not just cut down all the trees but engages in replanting them will continue to earn income from this source in the future.

Developing the economy is one way of ensuring environmental protection. Two classes of economic or commercial agents have been responsible for ruining the environment of land, air and water.

Big industrialists have dug up land and have excavated quarries leaving behind ugly sites that repel tourists. Hills covered in vegetation are a delight to look at, not bare rocks. Industrialists set up factories from which they may carelessly release waste into rivers. This effluent goes on to kill living things further downstream. Children bathe in or drink this water and their health suffers.

Air pollution takes a variety of forms. Smoke from factories puts too much carbon dioxide and other dangerous elements into the atmosphere. People breathe in this contaminated air and develop lung diseases. Noisy factories can damage the eardrums of people.

Garbage is found rotting everywhere in high density townships. It pollutes ground water sources. Without access to clean water the health of people suffers. Where health deteriorates, so will wealth. Garbage spreads disease. It should not be tolerated but removed and burnt immediately to kill pathogens.

Loss of biodiversity (the number of living organisms found in the same environment) can mean loss of new drugs. Our traditional healers depend on the herbs and tree barks that they find in the forests. When the woodland has been depleted of vegetation species it may mean loss of useful drugs. Even modern pharmaceutical companies look to the forests for some of their elements.

While the main despoilers of the environment are local people, such hazards as global warming originate in industrial countries.

Who is to ensure that development and the environment receive equal attention? While it is true that major industrial concerns these days have become more socially responsible, it is an indisputable fact that they put their own interests to the forefront. The State should therefore take upon itself the role of protector of the environment. Individuals and institutions will have to be involved, but the primary responsibility must lie with the State.

An approach to the small man who destroys the environment should be made through the local leader or authority whom the local man respects. This is the role of the village headman or chief. Government should provide incentives to these leaders so that they organise their people for local development plus preservation of the environment.

Any talk of poverty alleviation will ring hollow unless it includes activities that promote communal sanitation and clean drinking and laundry water, enriching instead of impoverishing the land. If short-term rising incomes entail the erosion of soils and flash floods due to the destruction of forests, you cannot say there has been development.

Where some people earn fat incomes working in factories or on farms whilst other people in the vicinity breathe polluted air, drink contaminated water, and die of industrial diseases, not much good is being achieved.

23 June 2003

REVITALISING THE ECONOMY

That the Malawi economy is growing at a snail's pace no honest person would cavil against. The problem is finding the solution. What can we do to accelerate growth to an extent that poverty eradication would become a reality instead of a pious dream?

As our own strategies and methods do not seem to take us very far it is time we started looking closely at the countries that have in the past few decades experienced impressive economic development. These countries in some sense must resemble our own. On top of the list I put Taiwan. Of the Tigers of the Far East, Taiwan is of most interest to us for more reasons than one. It is in size comparable to Malawi, larger in population but smaller geographically.

When such countries grow economically and prosper it is partly because they have succeeded in producing and manufacturing products for major markets abroad. For them autarky is out of the question. At the height of the Cold War, Taiwan forged strong economic links with the United States.

Though Korea has made dazzling records, and at the moment has the fastest growing economy in the Far East, we cannot easily and fruitfully imitate its large-scale industries such as shipping and car manufacturing. Taiwan grew out of small and medium-scale industries. Our hope lies in that direction.

Following the 11 September 2001 events, Taiwan's trade relations with the American market suffered just as did those of other countries. The 2003 outbreak of Severe Acute Respiratory Syndrome (Sars) added to the problems. Both had an effect on Taiwan's electronics, consumer and service industries. But the Taiwan authorities are by no means passive in their reaction to their economic disturbance. How they propose to contain the situation is a matter for us to study closely and relate to our even greater economic decline.

In the *Taiwan Journal* of 30 May 2003 there is an article by Francis Li headed *Chen creates new economic advisory body*. We are informed that on 23 May 2003 President Chen met leaders of Taiwan's six major industrial and commercial associations and three think-tanks. At the meeting, President Chen announced the formation of a presidential economic advisory panel to handle the economic fallout of Sars. Two matters of immediate interest to us should be noted at the outset. First, one of the associations invited was titled the National Association of Small and Medium Enterprises.

Do we have a parallel organisation specifically catering for the interests of smaller businesses? We need a national association of small-business people to encourage self-employment and the growth in production capacity, skills and entrepreneurship. After all, the fact that our agricultural industry is manned mostly by peasants and smallholder farmers means we are already used to small-scale enterprises. It is important that we move up into secondary industries. The tertiary field is already brimful with countless individual vendors.

Malawi needs a strong and fully representative body for small to medium-scale business people. On the Government side there should be a parallel organisation. The two in partnership would be constantly consulting with each other on the technological, commercial and financial problems of the self-employed entrepreneurs. Take for example the question of financing for smaller businesses. We are aware that the mainstream banks do not look kindly on applications for loans from the small man. Interest rates are also prohibitive. But is there a way out? An English saying is that, 'where there is a will, there is a way.' Problems do not depart by grousing about them. There has to be positive action.

While the formation of such an association is essentially a matter for private initiative, a helping hand from government, NGOs and donors would not be a bad proposition. I have for some time felt that some of the donor funds which go into bolstering one-man 'human rights' NGOs could be better diverted to cultural and economic enterprises that can benefit many.

The second point to note is that President Chen appointed a member of the opposition KMT, Vincent Siew, to serve as convener. This former premier will provide names of panel members to the presidential office, including academics, entrepreneurs and professionals. It is said Siew was appointed on the basis of his talents and experience. The fact that he is on the opposite side politically was not seen to be a problem in appointing him.

Where a national cause has arisen, a nation makes best use of its most capable citizens regardless of party affiliations. This is a point most politicians in Malawi find hard to embrace. When a member of the opposition is seen in conversation with a Minister of State or the President, the immediate conclusion is that he is being bought. Jealousy blinds some vocal people to the dire needs of the country. Multi-party politics is not intended to create enemies out of us. Where the national interest is uppermost, appointments should be strictly on merit.

We must all be constantly watching what other nations are doing so that we can learn from them. Vincent Siew in his report suggested to the government they look to the legendary New Deal of former US President, Franklin Roosevelt. This was put in place in 1933 to rescue the US economy from the Great Depression that followed the 1929 stock market crash in New York.

We could possibly profit by studying what the Taiwanese are currently doing to reinvigorate their economy. They are to put extra strength into agriculture, targeting major products such as mangoes and orchids. They also are planning surveys of traditional industries. Vice-Premier Lin was quoted as saying that the greatest problem the Taiwanese administration is facing is "implementing these policies". Perhaps in Malawi this problem is even greater.

There has never been a shortage of ideas in our press advocating fresh approaches to our economic problems. Some suggestions sound like plain nonsense, others have been more practical. But is there a mechanism for sorting out the grain from the chaff? Exactly who has the overall responsibility for implementing promising ideas?

<u>25 August 2003</u>

IS AID A HINDRANCE?

The years following World War II witnessed three events of enduring significance in international affairs. First was the quickening tempo towards colonial freedom. In 1947 Britain's jewel in the crown achieved independence as two separate states, India and Pakistan. In Africa, Sudan attained independence from the joint rule of Britain and Egypt in 1956, but the really momentous event was the independence of Ghana in 1957. Then followed a decade when Britain and France, who had been the main rivals in the scramble for Africa, now competed in granting self-rule to their colonies.

Secondly, this also became the period when the world came to talk of less-developed or developing countries. Most of these were former colonies, though some, such as Latin American countries, had been independent for almost a century. During the colonial era each colonial power was introducing elements of development to suit its own needs. Colonies had been founded to benefit the mother country primarily by the production and export to them of raw materials. The mother country then sent to the colonies manufactured goods, administrators, doctors and soldiers.

For a long time British economic policy was that each colony should pay its way rather than be subsidised by the British Treasury. Those colonies where valuable minerals were discovered, such as Northern Rhodesia (Zambia), experienced a measure of prosperity. This prosperity, however, impacted only peripherally on the indigenous people.

The third event was the start of what have become today's aid programmes. The British Colonial Office, with the advent of the Labour Government of Mr Clement Attlee, set up a fund for the development of colonies under the Colonial Development and Welfare Act. Development under the Act was subject to the budgetary constraints of the mother country. Britain had been ruined economically by Hitler's war.

It was only with the advent of independence that former colonies were open to aid and investment from countries other than their mother countries. Development aid arrived in different forms. It took the forms of capital grants or loans. The newly independent countries wanted to improve their physical infrastructure of railways, roads and bridges to facilitate investment in agriculture and industry. Assistance would be given to a country in the procurement of equipment and personnel for projects.

Though some of these countries were exporting cash crops such as tea, cocoa and tobacco plus minerals, they were not earning enough to save and invest in development projects. So they asked for aid in the procurement of capital goods. These goods could only be paid for in hard currencies such as dollars and pounds.

Aid came also in the form of technical assistance. Campaigners for independence had been promising their people better social services such as health and education. A developed country would send doctors to work in a developing country where the host government would pay a local salary in its own currency whilst the donor country added an inducement element in the currency of the expatriate's home country. In this way the developing country would have access to the services of highly qualified personnel without having to pay them salaries at international rates.

With the advent of independence rich countries competed in the provision of scholarships for students to study abroad. African students who had hitherto gone to Britain and France almost exclusively for higher education now went to West Germany, the Soviet Union and the United States. There they received higher education at no expense to their own governments or parents. This was technical assistance involving the transfer of knowledge rather than goods.

Development aid has settled into two categories, distinct but not quite independent of each other. There is bilateral aid, which takes place between one country and another. When Britain trains Malawian policemen without the Malawian Government meeting the cost, this is bilateral aid. Aid is multilateral when a group of countries contribute to a fund from which a developing country receives assistance. Examples are the European Union (EU) and the United Nations agencies, such as the World Bank.

Since the collapse of the Soviet Union, differences between bilateral and multilateral aid have become less pronounced. A developing country that fails to receive the sympathies of an individual donor is unlikely to be more successful with a multilateral agency. Bilateral aid givers are the major contributors to multilateral agencies. They see to it that the terms of bilateral and multilateral assistance do not differ much. A country that fails to meet the conditions of an individual donor cannot make a breakthrough with multilateral agencies

Dear Anne

I hope you enjoy the Au Plaisir book!

Judy

With Compliments

either. Donors have often told capital-starved countries such as Malawi that unless they satisfy the terms stipulated by the World Bank and IMF, they will not receive the funds that have been pledged. The days of playing one aid donor off against another are long gone.

While aid may be in the form of a direct grant requiring no repayment, quite often it is in the form of soft loans. A loan may be given at very low interest rates when compared with the rates the recipient country would pay in world financial markets. The loan may also be repayable over a period as long as 40 years, with a grace period of five years.

While most aid is between governments, some of it comes through charitable bodies generally known as non-governmental organisations (NGOs). For a long time, both in aid-giving and aid-receiving countries, some people have questioned the benefits of aid to the receiver and to the donor.

One would assume that the benefits are obvious when the United States or Britain sends food to a starving African nation. But some people have pointed out that the US sends out yellow and genetically-modified (GM) maize to African countries to pave the way for its own agricultural exports. In other words, rarely is aid a matter of pure altruism.

Aid has often been given to influence the politics of a developing nation. This was particularly so during the Cold War era. With the end of the Cold War, aid givers compel applicants for assistance to adopt democratic ideals and to open their countries to foreign investors and traders. But this is done at the same time these donor countries are erecting tariff and non-tariff barriers against the exports of these same developing countries. In international relationships, inconsistencies abound.

Both in developed and developing countries there are people who say aid encourages a dependency mentality in developing countries. Instead of doing the maximum to help themselves, leaders of developing countries prefer to go abroad cap in hand seeking aid.

15 September 2003

THOUGHTS ON POPULATION

When you point a finger at someone, note that three fingers point at you from your own hand as if to remind you that while there is a speck of dust in someone else's eye, there is a beam in your own. The Minister of Health and Population, Hon Yusuf Mwawa, is reported in *The Nation* of 11 September 2003 as lamenting the fact that despite Government and NGO appeals, people are having more children than government can support with health services.

Overpopulation is not just a health hazard. It is more of an economic burden. Time and time again one has heard someone saying Malawians are poorer now than they were 10 years ago. This is said to be the fault of those who are running the government. Only up to a point is this true.

In all discussions about developing this country we must not shy away from reminding ourselves of our collective responsibility. Government cannot solve most of people's problems unless the people themselves play a major role. If God helps those who help themselves, how can government succeed in helping those who do not do anything about their own problems?

Appeals for birth control have always provoked derision, if not anger. Because Thomas Malthus (1766–1834) of Cambridge University in his book *An Essay on the Principle of Population* (1798) gave warning about the tendency of population growth to outpace the means of subsistence, his critics denounced economics as the dismal science, the science that prompted gloom and dismay.

Hardly any textbook on economics today forgets to say something about population and to refer to Malthus. Many writers continue to say that Malthus underestimated the capacity for technological growth which made it possible for industrial Europe and North America to accommodate larger populations at higher standards of living.

The truth is that the dire consequences of which Malthus wrote did not take place not just because of advances in technology. In the 18th century large migrations of people from Europe to other continents began. It is there that pressure on the means of subsistence resulted in the survival of the fittest and extinction of the weak. It is possibly correct to say that at the time of Christopher Columbus, both North and South America had populations of native Indians larger than they have now. Later, wars were fought in Europe and abroad for *lebensraum* (living space) as Hitler put it.

Today there is reverse migration. People from developing countries, even from the supposedly rich Middle East, are scrambling to reach the shores of the European Union and North America. It is heart-rending to learn that West Africans have drowned in the Mediterranean whilst being illegally ferried from North Africa to Italy or France. Mugabe's economic policies have so impoverished his people that they are now among the thousands who find their way to the UK in search of jobs.

The continuing poverty of Africa must be partly blamed on those who disregard family planning. As someone has said, whoever fails to plan, plans to fail. Economic planning must include family planning. No matter how many plans the government puts in place, if the population grows regardless, whatever economic growth is attained will simply fail to raise people's living standards. If standards of living have not improved in the last 10 years, it is partly because the population has been increasing at a faster rate than the GDP.

In industrial countries it is poor and agricultural families that tend to have many children. Rich couples divert their earnings to pet dogs and extra cars once they have a couple of children. It is doubtful if the middle classes in Africa have started to do much about family planning.

Those in authority, together with NGOs, should use simple messages to try and reach the people's conscience. The latter must be asked: where will your extra children find the land to cultivate? Where will they find jobs? Not beyond the Zambezi. People in Harare and Jubeki are themselves going abroad in search of jobs. If your salary is not adequate for the children you already have, then how will you bring up the extra children that keep on coming?

The effects of overpopulation are already being seen. When budgets for the Ministries of Health and Education are increased, we continue to hear complaints of clinics lacking drugs, dilapidated hospitals, classrooms without desks and secondary school students being taught by primary school teachers.

Politics in Malawi attracts self-righteous participants who talk as if they themselves could solve the present problems the moment power is transferred to them. The fact is that our cultural beliefs, compounded with certain religious beliefs, are at the heart of our economic handicaps. These must be updated.

The truth must be brought home to people. It is not the duty of the State to feed families or to bring up their children. Each family must try hard to support itself. The State is there to help, not to take over these responsibilities.

Among the stumbling blocks to keeping the population within limits are religious fanatics. Five years ago at a world conference on population in Cairo, some faith leaders vehemently opposed proposals on control methods put forward by some American delegates. These people must know that economic and social problems cannot be solved by emotionalism.

It may be immoral to terminate the foetus, but when populations exceed the means of subsistence, people fight wars. The constant killings seen in the Great Lakes region are not purely ethnic. They have to do with the struggle for land and jobs. When God urged Abraham to multiply his family like stars, the earth was empty. Now it is brim-full.

Economic development will start showering benefits on people when birth rates lag behind GDP growth rates and not vice-versa. This will come about when chiefs, politicians, priests, pastors, sheikhs and other leaders speak the same language on population.

28 November 2003

ECONOMIC PHILOSOPHY, PERFORMANCE

On the day I started working on this essay, 20 November 2003, I heard on the radio that the world was celebrating the discipline called philosophy. Economic philosophy deals with the objectives of economic activities and the methods that are considered rational for achieving these objectives.

Following President Muluzi's statement on the performance of his first government on 18 October 2003, there was a chorus of criticism from the opposition and pressure groups linked with faiths. The leader of the opposition in Parliament pulled no punches, while the spokesman of a Synod demanded that Dr Muluzi should apologise to the nation for the alleged sufferings he has inflicted on the country.

Were these criticisms fair? A good deal depends on whether they were in conformity with Malawi's economic philosophy. The question then is: does Malawi have an economic philosophy? Yes, though not explicit. Because there is vagueness about our economic philosophy the criticisms are sometimes misplaced. While some are valid, others are self-righteous.

Malawi subscribes to the economic philosophy known variously as free enterprise or capitalism, that is, a market economy. Under this philosophy individuals and bodies corporate are free to engage in business and to own property such as shops, buses, banks, schools and hospitals.

The role of the State is only vaguely defined in this country, where political parties are devoid of ideologies. John Maynard Keynes said the State should not do things that people are already doing, but should do those which no one else is doing. Because people are already engaged in a business there is no point in the State also engaging in that business. Therefore, sell government-owned enterprises; privatise.

Has the government acted wisely in engaging in privatisation? Could some enterprises have been left under State control without loss of profits or deterioration of services?

It is self-defeating to make blanket criticism, for you may be criticising the public sector for failures that ought to be attributed to the private sector. The State has a duty to provide free primary education. Has it also the duty to erect every school building in the country and to equip it with desks and exercise books? Is it entirely the government's fault that some children learn whilst sitting under trees?

If the answer is yes, then be prepared to provide the government with extra money through taxation. Do not grumble about the ubiquitous surtax because the State is trying to raise the extra income it has foregone by abolishing the poll and some personal taxes. It is a sign of immaturity to grumble about everything under the sun.

Nothing is completely free in life except the air we breathe. When you ask the State to do more for you, you are indirectly advocating the economic philosophy known as dirigisme, socialism or communism. Taxes are high under any one of these systems.

A study of economic history reveals that the role of the State has been to provide the conditions under which private enterprise can flourish. Most inventions that changed economies in the past were not made by civil servants. Marconi, who invented wireless telephony in 1901 and thereby inaugurated modern electronic media, was not a government employee. Thomas Edison, who invented the incandescent electric lamp, was not a civil servant either. If we go back to the beginnings of the Industrial Revolution in Britain, we see that the inventions which fuelled this phenomenon were all made by non-State employees.

Without inventions and innovation a country cannot make much progress in economic development and in attaining higher standards of living. Japan and Taiwan started by imitating the products and industrial techniques of the West, but went on to introduce their own modifications and innovations.

How have we, the private people of Malawi, fared in this game of invention and innovation? Nowadays there are numerous graduates in physics, chemistry and other branches of learning which form the basis of invention and innovation. But we see little evidence of results. Has the State created situations where our scientists have found it impossible to invent a chemical that would purify tobacco of those elements which damage health? Is it that the State has made it impossible for corporations or individuals to find new uses for maize, millet, cassava, wood and groundnuts such as would have introduced new industries into the economy?

Industrialisation takes place where there is genuine partnership between the private and public sectors. The best partnership is that where each partner brings in the expertise that other partners do not have. The partners then complement, rather than duplicate each other.

Some people in Malawi believe that being a perpetual critic of the Government is the best way to serve the country. They ignore President John Kennedy's dictum: "Ask not what your country can do for you – ask what you can do for your country." Wanton criticism is destructive. It demoralises and builds nothing.

Malawi is economically a miserable country with its unfavourable trade and payment balances and its hovering inflation. The majority of its people live below the international poverty line. But if we say it is exclusively the fault of those of who have been running public affairs for the past nine years we miss the opportunity to discover the real causes. We are like people who, when there are outbreaks of pestilence in the community, look out for witches to blame instead of the real causes.

If Muluzi has to apologise, he must apologise for those economic hardships in Malawi that can be traced to government policies. For example, the government has committed Malawi to the regional economic groupings of SADC and COMESA. If these relationships have brought benefits, Muluzi must be congratulated, if they have retarded the Malawi economy, he must be criticised. Critics should then be specific in pointing out the costs and benefits; how much better or worse off would we have been if we had not joined these economic groupings.

I do not deny that Malawi's stagnant economy is partly the fault of the State. But it must be repeated that we of the private sector have also under-performed. We have not invented, we have not innovated and we have not organised ourselves for competitiveness in this age of globalisation.

A change of government and president will not of itself make a difference to this country's economic plight. We must discard cultural habits that are inimical to economic success. We must cultivate a work ethic. Those who say that all our problems can be solved by the State are misleading the public.

THE ECONOMICS AND QUALITY OF EDUCATION

The biographers of Robert Laws, the first missionary to achieve impressive results in this country in the late 19th century, tell us that he was guided by a German saying: "What you want to have in the country, first put in the schools."

Dr Laws did not just want to prepare African Christians for a place in paradise; he also wanted them to cope with a modern world of industry, science, technology and civil service. At the Overtoun Institute, Livingstonia, he introduced a curriculum that included theology, artisanship, printing, commercial studies, medicine, agriculture and, of course, academic education plus teacher training.

Missionaries who came after him adopted a similar or modified curriculum. The result was that during the first half of the 20th century Malawi was producing better educated and better trained Africans than neighbouring countries.

The Nyasa teacher, clerk, carpenter or medical auxiliary was in demand by employers from Durban to Dar es Salaam. All these results were achieved in the days when this country was as relatively poor as it is now. The secret was in making the best use of the resources that you have to get what you want.

We Malawians of today must also begin by stating unequivocally what it is that we want to have in this country. Having done that, we must first put it in schools. Education is the starting point. When things go wrong with the education system other systems suffer as well.

As has been stated again and again, the leaders of our political parties have much in common as to what they want to do if put in power. They all talk about alleviating or even eradicating poverty, they talk of creating new jobs, providing justice and good governance. What people have to choose is not the ideology of one party vis-à-vis that of another, but the personality of one leader as against that of another. In short, all participants in public life agree that without economic development, all talk about poverty alleviation is simply worthless.

But how much of what we want must we put in our schools? As individuals and as a nation it pays to study the ways of great achievers. In the field of modern economic development one must turn one's eyes to South East Asia and the Pacific Rim for models. In *The Economist*, 13 December 2003, under the heading *Banking on education to propel a new spurt of growth*, we read of the priority that countries such as Malaysia, Thailand and Singapore give to education.

Before retiring, the Malaysian Prime Minister, Mahathir Mohamad, made education the centrepiece of his final year. His Thai counterpart has made great efforts to improve local schools. In Singapore officials speak of little else but the knowledge society and lifelong learning. There is no doubt that education has been a key factor in taking Singapore from the third world to the first, to borrow a phrase from the autobiography of its first Prime Minister, Lee Kuan Yew.

In Malawi we must be asking ourselves, 'with the resources that we have, what must we put in our schools that can help propel our country from the third world to at least the second?' We must not dwell on excuses. The fact that we are a small country does not mean we cannot develop. Singapore, Taiwan and Mauritius have achieved impressive results without being extensive geographical areas.

Are we putting into our schools the type of curriculum that can act as an engine of economic growth? Have we looked at what the Singaporeans, the Taiwanese and the Japanese teach in their schools which may have contributed to their wealth and well-being? How do we compare our MSCE core subjects with those of Singapore? Can a Malawian student who passes the MSCE with distinction also pass the Taiwanese equivalent with distinction? When we talk of giving this country quality education, what benchmark or model do we have in mind?

From the same issue of *The Economist* we learn that Singaporean students top the tables in international comparisons of students in mathematics and science subjects. Two-thirds or more of all children in the Philippines, Malaysia, Thailand and Vietnam attend secondary schools. How does this compare with attendance in Malawi?

What must we teach in our schools? When we read of the SADC and COMESA economic groupings we sometimes assume that these bodies have no precedents. In fact, they have. During colonial days, those European countries which had colonies in Africa south of the Sahara used to hold regular conferences to compare their programmes and policies.

Perhaps the last of these conferences was held in Dar es Salaam in 1959. Tanganyika was then a self-governing country but not yet independent. The 37-year-old Prime Minister, Mwalimu Julius Nyerere, opened the conference with words that have failed to desert my memory. He said: "A research scientist may be interested in finding out why a fish that is grey in colour turns blue when taken out of water, but what has that to do with our problems here?" In other words, education and research must relate to the problems of a specific country.

A good deal of debate is about the decline in the quality of education in Malawi. Some people think that this decline started with the introduction of free primary education in 1994. This is not so. The decline started earlier. At a number of public rallies as well as in Parliament Dr Banda, the President, used to compare unfavourably the type of primary education being provided in schools during his time as president with the type of primary education he had received.

It is almost in the nature of things that when you provide mass education, whether at primary or other levels, standards fall somewhere. With the resources available let us have at least five secondary schools which can provide top-quality education, as do the French. To these schools we should send the best teachers and the best students. We should try to create an educated élite within which we might discover innovators and inventors. It is these few people who lead forward the development of civilisation.

But, we must let every child have access to high-quality and universal primary education.

26 January 2004

IS FAMINE COMING AGAIN?

More than 10 years ago the Sahelian countries of Mali, Burkina Faso and Niger suffered famine for nearly seven years. Cattle and other domestic beasts died of thirst and hunger. At the same time, in this part of Africa, we had good rains; not many people were dying of starvation.

For the past five years or so it has been the turn of southern Africa to experience prolonged drought and famine. This rainy season we understand that even South Africa may experience food shortfalls because of inadequate rains.

This is unfortunate. The SADC region cannot afford another Zimbabwe scenario, where confiscation of land from white farmers happened at a time when the country was experiencing poor rains. The famine in Zimbabwe had both natural and socio-political causes.

Apparently some people in southern Africa have learned nothing from Zimbabwe's economic chaos. In Namibia we understand some land-hungry citizens are threatening to seize white-owned farms in the same manner as in Zimbabwe. In South Africa senior government officials have threatened white farmers who refuse to surrender their land to government for redistribution to landless blacks.

Whilst injustices of the past must be reversed, this must be done without inflicting undue suffering on third parties. When land is seized from one class of society and given to another it is better that total food production be at least maintained at the old level. If following such land seizures food production falls and many people starve, then the redistribution of land has not been done properly. Perhaps the new owners of the land are not committed farmers, in which case they do not deserve to hold on to the land.

Erratic rains may be heralding another year or two of food shortage, but a desperate situation need not arise if those running the affairs of the State are better organised.

From what we learn it is only in the Southern Region that rains are unsatisfactory whilst in the rest of the country there is no cause for concern. We should, therefore, work out our strategy so that the harvest shortfalls in the south can be met from the surpluses of other regions. After all, the Central Region has been the granary of the country for a good part of our history.

Instead of dishing out largesse in the form of tonnes of maize at political rallies we should be distributing farm inputs in those parts of the country where the rains are good. Give a person a dish of rice or *nsima* today and he will remain content only for the time the food remains in his stomach. When he is hungry again and you stop giving him more food he will start grumbling. Give a family a basket of maize, that family will remain happy so long as there are grains in the basket

They are a rare breed of people who remember yesterday's banquet when they are hungry today. The Biblical Hebrews or children of Israel nearly revolted against Moses in the Sinai Desert during the brief time they had little to eat.

Government should empower the people to feed themselves. Those of the regions with normal rains should feed the whole country. It is better to spend cash now to achieve higher yields instead of having to import maize later.

To encourage people to grow more maize there should be an economic or commercial incentive. People are no longer satisfied with merely having enough food; they want to have enough money to buy those things that have become conventional necessities, such as better clothes, radios and education of their children. At a time like this the government should announce the better prices it is going to pay for the maize to be brought to markets next harvest. Give people a price incentive to produce more and they will produce more. In the past such offers were made through Admarc.

We hear now and again Members of Parliament echoing the State President in appealing to the people to plant the drought-resistant crops cassava and potatoes. However, this must be supported by assisting people in obtaining the necessary cuttings or seedlings. It is wrong to assume that everyone has the seeds or seedlings readily at hand. Supplement words with action. "Do not expect what you do not inspect," said W. Clement Stone, the American multi-millionaire. When you have appealed to the people to grow drought-resistant crops, visit them to find out if they are doing so, and if not, why not.

Heart-warming promises are never in short supply in this country. It is purposeful action that one sees lacking. When Aleke Banda was Minister of Agriculture and Irrigation he put into practice the principles of Peter F. Drucker, i.e. Management by Objectives (MBO). He would call a meeting of all those concerned with agriculture such as farmers, extension officers, donors and suppliers of inputs. He would invite them to affirm what they could do to help the country produce adequate food. All these good people would point out what they were doing and the problems they faced. After four months or so they would attend another workshop to review the progress made. In this way all stakeholders in farming were kept working towards a common goal.

Unfortunately, in this case, Management by Objectives was followed by Management by Political Objection. A competent minister who two years earlier had piloted the country to food surpluses was no longer available to continue his good work.

How do famines come about, you ask. Part of the answer is found in politics. It is not me saying this, but Nobel Prize laureate in economics, Amartya Sen. The political élite who are not facing starvation at the household level have different priorities in the struggle against yearly famine. After all, some of them make more money from their commercial deals when the country is short of food than when it has bumper harvests.

The attainment of permanent food security will require the cooperation of agricultural experts, nutritionists, chemists and those in the catering industry. Our ancestors were very inventive about food. They did not just eat *nsima* from maize but also from cassava and millet. They brewed beer from a variety of raw materials. Why do modern Malawians feel they have not had lunch or dinner unless there is *nsima* in the dish?

Nutritionists and restaurants should try to introduce dishes of cassava and potatoes which could substitute maize *nsima*. Malawi awaits a George Washington Carver.

27 January 2004

OBJECTIVES OF GENERAL ELECTIONS

"**M**an is born free and everywhere he is in chains," wrote Jean-Jacques Rousseau in *The Social Contract.* "Workers of the world unite, you have nothing to lose but your chains," wrote Marx and Engels in *The Communist Manifesto.* "Truth shall make you free," said Jesus Christ according to the Gospel of St John.

Is man now free since these great sages made their utterances? Perhaps some feel free, but not all. The struggle to be free still continues. To be alive is to be dissatisfied. You throw away the chains of the slave master only to wear other chains. Some people won freedom from colonial rule only to be ensnared in home-made tyranny.

There is great excitement about the May 2004 presidential and parliamentary elections. Some people have already confirmed their names on the electoral roll, some have registered for the first time, others are reminded to go and register. Do we all have the same motives for going to vote? Not likely.

No political situation is loved or hated by everyone. Any reform that takes place injures some people whilst benefiting others. During the struggle for independence between 1954 and 1964 most of us looked forward to the day we would enjoy a fuller kind of life. But when independence came things did not turn out rosy for some people.

There were those who fled the country and lived in exile for thirty years. There were those who were imprisoned or killed. At that time, some of those who had been mere clerks were transformed into senior administrative officers; some became chauffeur-driven cabinet ministers, living in houses formerly occupied by senior colonial officials.

The attainment of multi-party democracy in 1993–4 was hailed by millions as a dawn of better times, a reformation. But those who had privileges during the MCP/Kamuzu era had little to celebrate. What they had, they lost.

The present political situation shows as many dissatisfied people as the previous one. We have people who display almost pathological disenchantment with the way the country is being run. Openly they are calling upon the masses of the people not to vote for the party currently in power.

People who are saying such things are acting within their rights so far as the Constitution goes, but a caveat must be thrown in here. When you discard your present spouse and marry another you do not necessarily attain celestial bliss. You have to be as careful as ever in choosing your next wife or husband.

There are those people who in the way they write, speak or preach seem to suggest that a government formed by any other party would be preferable to the current one. Not necessarily. Let us make sure we are not jumping out of a sinking boat only to land in the mouth of a crocodile.

Those who have taken it upon themselves to educate the masses as to how to exercise their voting rights should remind the people that the crucial choice is not between political parties but presidential candidates. There is hardly any ideological difference between one political party and another. We have to decide between the personalities and credentials of one presidential candidate and those of another.

Malawi has definitely attained three or four of the five freedoms that President Franklin Roosevelt proclaimed at the beginning of World War II. These were the freedoms of association, speech and religion, and freedom from fear. What is eluding Malawi is freedom from want. Poverty follows us like our shadow. It is with us at midday; it is with us at midnight.

From among the several persons who will be vying for the post of President, people should cast their vote for someone who has the capability of rescuing them from economic stagnation. Voting for a party and voting for a President should be treated as separate processes. Let us follow the example of people in the United States and France.

If a person sees that his favourite party has fielded a candidate of doubtful credentials, he should vote for someone else, even if that one belongs to a rival party. Do not vote for a deficient candidate just because he belongs to your party. If through his defects he fails to make this country economically better off, or introduces the old-style politics of detentions and murders, we all are bound to suffer. Put the interests of the country above those of the party.

What sort of person would make a competent President? Recently, some people have suggested that a Presidential candidate should have at least a bachelor's degree. While it is true that a poorly educated person cannot effectively guide a modern state, it is a fallacy to assume that only men with degrees can make good presidents, or to think that because someone has a PhD he would make an even better President.

Some of the greatest statesmen we know had no university degrees. Churchill failed to pass the equivalent of a General Certificate of Education and so did not go to Oxford. Yet he was a greater statesman than Attlee, a lawyer. Nearer home there was Kenneth Kaunda who ruled Zambia for almost 27 years.

In his autobiography, *Long Walk to Freedom*, Dr Nelson Mandela tells us he worked with non-graduates who were more competent and spoke better English than some graduates. This immediately reminds us of Tom Mboya of Kenya, Dunduzu Chisiza of Malawi and Clements Kadalie who organised workers in South Africa. They were all brilliant orators and organisers.

What is required of a President is a fertile mind – a mind that can learn new things in this kaleidoscopic world of change. A President should read books and magazines and surround himself with people who can strengthen his intellect.

A Presidential candidate should have a good reputation. He should be willing to answer questions about his past record, in office and outside. Many of those who will be voting next May were mere primary school children during the previous era. They do not know much about the forthcoming presidential candidates, their deeds or misdeeds. They ought to know.

Whoever does not want his past to be discussed should withdraw from the presidential race. Malawians are tired of public relations orators, they want reformers. They want prosperity in place of poverty. We must have a competent person, but one who has never victimised his political opponents.

16 February 2004

WHY IS AFRICA POOR?

O n the front cover of *The Economist* dated 17 January 2004 there is a photograph of an African girl, well-dressed (for a change) with a sari flowing from the back of her head to the bottom of the page. I have said well-dressed for a change because overseas magazines love to represent Africans with the most wretched of their specimens.

Inside the magazine is a 14-page report on sub-Saharan Africa headed: *How to make Africa smile.* The cover girl's smile hints at some weariness. It is the smile of someone who has perhaps been crying for some time. In this sense the picture is truly representative of our continent.

There is something to celebrate in Africa but it is not possible to flash out a prolonged smile in the world's second largest continent because painful events and disturbing news are always just around the corner. The report says of Africa: "Even more worryingly it is the only continent to have grown poorer in the past 25 years despite the explosion of technologies."

Half a century ago, as both colonial Africa and Asia were marching towards independence, world commentators were giving Africa as a whole a brighter future, in terms of realising an economic take-off, than Asia. Sub-Saharan Africa had abundant resources of minerals, oil and fertile soils; and its population was a good deal lower than that of India and China. Africa did indeed look as if it would conquer its poverty in less than a couple of decades. But as it has turned out, Asia has done better despite its poorer natural resources. The explanation can only be found in human resources.

The writer of the report, Robert Guest, says Africa remains poor mainly because of bad governments. To what extent is our guest speaker correct? Have Asian governments been a good deal better than African governments? We know for sure that there have been dictatorships amongst them. In some Asian countries prime ministers have been assassinated and corruption on a grand scale has been unearthed. And yet Asia has developed faster than Africa. The reasons must be complex. We must, however, start with bad governance.

Only Botswana comes out clean from the international auditing of Africa.

Since changing its name from Bechuanaland to Botswana on independence in the 1960s, the largely desert country has enjoyed multi-party democracy plus the chance discovery of diamonds, which has given it one of the highest per capita income growths in the world.

There are other countries in Africa where precious reserves of oil and minerals have been unearthed, but their rulers' idea has been that if you have the power then amass the property, deposit the cash in Swiss banks and buy villas on the Mediterranean coast. Mobuto Sese Seko and Sani Abacha are two examples and so many of Africa's leaders have indulged in the same dirty game.

But some African leaders are innocent of self-aggrandisement. Nyerere did not die opulent and no one has accused the ascetic Presbyterian Kenneth Kaunda of having grown richer than his country.

What we have in Africa is economic stagnation, both in countries where there have been corrupt governments and in those governed by honest men. Bad governance must be one of the explanations for Africa's poverty, but not the only one. Corrupt princes did not prevent economic take-off in the now industrialised countries.

At the back of African poor performance is the culture. We Africans have learned to love the products of Western civilisation; the cars, the TVs, the immaculate clothes, but without pausing to learn the secrets of those countries that produce such goods. In Africa you are admired for looking opulent, not for success in matters that would help your country to prosper. Conspicuous consumption is the antithesis of the frugality and investment that would make an economy grow.

We must look into our culture. We do not have to subscribe to Max Weber's 'Protestant Ethic' because the achievers of the Far East are more Confucian than Calvinist. But they work harder and save more than we do here in Africa. Even in high school we hear of students in tiny Singapore outshining those of the West. We must self-scrutinise to find out what it is in our culture that is inimical to economic development. At the same time we must not underrate external constraints, especially in the relationships between developed and developing countries.

Up to 1960 these relationships were usually those of colonial master and colony. Colonies exported raw materials to the colonial master or tutor, the latter exported processed and manufactured products. These relationships have now crystallised into some that support and some which frustrate development. I refer to trade and aid relationships.

After receiving development aid for four decades or so, many African countries still show no sign of approaching prosperity. Many leaders and commentators say aid without trade cannot take their countries far on the road to development. But, in developed countries there are economic groups which resist imports from developing countries. Such groups include farmers, textile manufacturers and other industries whose production technologies are now possessed by developing countries.

African presidents who have brought their countries to virtual insolvency have then gone to the World Bank, IMF and other donors for bail-outs. In return, the latter have prescribed reforms that include balancing budgets, the privatisation of State industries and staff reductions in the civil service. These results have brought about pain, but as yet no visible gain. If these reforms are then to be abandoned, what shall we have in their place? Why are the reforms slow in bearing fruit? A Ghanaian economist, George Ayittey, has been quoted as saying that most IMF-sponsored reforms have amounted merely to reorganising a bankrupt company and then placing it, complete with massive infusions of capital, in the hands of the same incompetent managers who ruined it in the first place.

If only Malawians who are to cast their vote in May could reflect on this. Some of the candidates aspiring to the presidency were in the government before. If they failed to perform in the past, what reason do we have to believe they could this time bring about the desirable changes?

Whether during the next five years Malawi becomes poorer or more prosperous will depend very much on who we choose to be our next president. A person who is hard-working and totally committed to the nation is more likely to bring into his team people like him. This is the person the country needs. We need a results-oriented leader; not someone who merely tells us what he will do, but someone who can show us what he has already done.

6 August 2004

FLEEING FROM MALAWI'S POVERTY

About a month ago a neighbour and church elder paid me a visit to discuss things spiritual. After the preliminary greetings my wife asked how our guest's madam was. He replied, "Ah, she has retired from her post as a matron and has gone to work in England. These days it is the women rather than the men who venture far to look for work."

I forgot about this until last week when, whilst reading *The Weekly Telegraph*, my eye caught a rare article in this type of paper headed: "Malawi left denuded as nurses head for Britain." The article was by David Blair from Lilongwe.

Above the heading was a photograph of women with young children sitting waiting for attention in Lilongwe Central Hospital. This hospital, I understand, to be fully operational needs 532 nurses; instead it has only 183. This not so much because the training of nurses in Malawi has remained inadequate, but because those who have qualified have left to seek better pay abroad. Since 2002 Malawi has lost 211 nurses. Says Blair: "One of the poorest nations has lost 9 per cent of all its nurses in the past two years, with 82 per cent going to Britain."

Not just nurses but other professionals and academicians have left this beloved country for those that offer them more compensation than they can earn at home. These professionals want to earn and save money whilst they are still young. Serving one's own interest is a natural right, provided that in doing so one does not harm the rights of other people. However, beyond self-interest there is public service. This we all owe our country, each according to our potential.

Malawi has been an exporter of manpower since the dawn of the 20th century. All the countries to which Malawian job-seekers went in droves, such as South Africa, Zimbabwe and Zambia, are economically more developed today, though they too are battling with the brain-drain. A doctor at the Lilongwe Central Hospital is reported to have lamented: "Instead of the British taking our nurses, why don't they give us money to improve working conditions here?"

I would not say the British have been cheese-paring whenever we have approached them for financial and technical help. Actually I think Britain has since 1964 subsidised Malawi more than when the country was a protectorate.

British colonial policy then was that each colony should pay its way instead of being a drain on the Exchequer. Indeed, when Harry Johnston began administering the Nyasaland Protectorate it was for some time subsidised by the Kimberley diamond millionaire, Cecil Rhodes.

Millions of British pounds have entered Malawi since the Union Jack left and yet Malawi remains poor and unattractive to some of its own trained professionals, particularly nurses and doctors. Though we cannot blame those who emigrate to seek greener pastures, we can still remind them of the facts of economic history.

Going abroad to a prosperous country offers only a temporary solution. Economic conditions never remain the same anywhere. Malawians are no longer being enticed to go and work in Zimbabwe and South Africa precisely because these countries are no longer as prosperous as they used to be. Their own people are now trekking in their thousands overseas to seek more remunerative employment.

In recent economic history perhaps no two countries have made such miraculous economic turnarounds as Germany and Japan. When I was in Germany 35 years ago I learned for the first time the term 'guest workers'. It was then a prosperous part of Europe. Nowadays magazines such as *The Economist* refer to Germany as the sick man of Europe, the epithet once applied to Britain in pre-Thatcherite days.

For a semi-permanent solution to the problem of this brain-drain and low pay we must accelerate the development of this country. Such development has, however, eluded us for so long that we sometimes lose hope that Malawi will ever be able to resign from the club of poor countries.

The accent has to be put on national will. This matters a good deal in a multi-party and democratic country. It is gratifying that so far the leaders of the MCP and Hon Justin Malewezi have said things that suggest they put the national interest above personal or partisan interest. The country will need more of this spirit as our new President, Bingu wa Mutharika, tackles the gargantuan task of transforming the economy of Malawi.

The freedom that democracy gives is sometimes abused by people who turn that freedom into a licence to frustrate honest endeavours by others to bring about desirable changes. There is no gainsaying that within the ranks of the UDF there is a cabal that wants to frustrate the new President's plans to introduce reforms. This clandestine group wishes Mutharika to put UDF interests above national interests. It forgets that Mutharika is a State president, not just a UDF president. Where national interest and party interest differ, the President should serve the national interest. Where it is clear that the measures he is introducing are necessary for economic growth, the whole nation should support him. There has to be the national willpower to succeed.

3 December 2004

ECONOMICS OF DEVELOPMENT: MALAWI

It is a fact that while possession of empires contributed to the industrialisation of Britain and France, it did not do so for Spain and Portugal.

Why some countries underwent industrial transformation earlier than others is one of the topics often discussed in the economics of development. Countries which obtained political unity and stability early generally proceeded to industrialise their economies early. Peace and political stability form the matrix for any meaningful development. The culture of the people also influenced the pace of economic and social development. Some cultures inhibit rather than propel development.

The role of minority groups in the development of countries is significant. Max Weber, the German sociologist, identified the role played by minority Protestant sects in the development of industries in Europe and North America. He talked of the Protestant or Calvinist ethic. Other economists have pointed out the role of the Jews in many countries, of the Chinese dwelling in other Asian countries and of the Asians in East and Central Africa. All these have contributed to the development of their adopted nations.

At the centre of development are the people. The absence of rich natural resources frustrates efforts to develop a country, but where people have the right motivation, development takes place. This is the economic history of Japan, Taiwan and Singapore.

Indians and the Chinese have engaged in trade on a large scale for centuries. Marco Polo, Vasco da Gama and Christopher Columbus headed for these countries in pursuit of trading opportunities. In contrast, the people of sub-Saharan Africa have only limited experience of large scale and international trading. It has been much easier for Indians and Chinese to go into the international field because entrepreneurs are there among them.

Malawi has been independent for exactly 40 years. Countries that were at the same level of under-development and poverty 40 years ago, such as Mauritius, Taiwan and Singapore, have now moved far ahead. When we peep into the history of the newly industrialised countries we notice that the role of the State was more than that of referee; it was more like that of a general or pilot. The State must be proactive rather than reactive.

If during the next five years this country is to experience faster economic development, then certain conditions must be fulfilled. One must be the attitude of people in office. They must go beyond just talking about development; they must do things that facilitate such development.

The State must be entrepreneurial. Having privatised certain of its industries, it must not hesitate to start fresh ones in sectors of the economy where private industry is rather timid. To privatise and then do nothing else but ensure law and order will not be enough. We do not have a plethora of entrepreneurs emerging out of mercantile business, as is the case with India and China. The State must act as an entrepreneur and create entrepreneurs.

President Mutharika shows a high commitment to development. His education in economics and his long experience in working for international institutions equip him well for success, provided he receives cooperation from all around him. At present there is little evidence of his receiving such cooperation. Those who had sponsored and supported his presidential candidature are now openly working to frustrate his efforts and to create a political climate that is inimical to investment and development.

Disgruntled men who did not make it to the cabinet and some with skeletons in their cupboards now say they regret their sponsorship. If they had the power, they would possibly seek to dethrone him. These people are guided solely by personal and party, not national, interests. They feel Mutharika should reward political party activists first before serving national interests. This attitude is sending the wrong signals to the donors on whom we depend so much for our budgetary and developmental support.

At the same time Mutharika should not ignore grumblers. There is no such thing as a small enemy. He should see to it that his henchmen do not provoke anyone, whether UDF or other party cadres.

Where Government property is missing, every effort should be made to trace it and, if it has been stolen, the perpetrators should be brought before the law. But investigations should not be made just for the purpose of embarrassing someone. I have in mind the calls made by some people to investigate the circumstances in which Dr Bakili Muluzi pardoned an Asian convicted of a crime. There are a number of other instances in which Muluzi released prisoners who deserved a longer stay. No one took him to task on these occasions.

I would remind the President that history will judge him by the type of regime that he sets up, not by how many culprits of the previous regime he rounds up. The President should sit in the driver's seat with his eyes looking ahead. He should close loopholes for all forms of malpractice, including nepotism, incompetence, regionalism and bribery.

The civil service is the largest sector of the economy. President Mutharika should give more time to improve the civil service than did his predecessor. He should moderate his commitments to international and regional conferences so that he may have more time for domestic problems. He would do well to follow the footsteps of Lee Kuan Yew and seek the advice of foreign experts in some of the problems facing the country. What can be done in five years should be done in 5 years and not be subjected to Parkinson's Law.

Malawi is in a state of emergency economically. Too many people are looking for jobs, too many are facing starvation. Mr President, be surrounded by men and women of genuine commitment.

In order that Mutharika should take the country forward, people of all political persuasions should rally behind him whenever he is carrying out projects that will help us all. In American politics, once a president has been installed he does not seem to be much involved with party matters. What matters is that members of Congress (US Parliament) are with him. If Mutharika is doing the right things, the media, NGOs and other persons of influence should publicly encourage him.

1959

Wind of
change
speech

4 February 2005

TONY BLAIR AND AFRICA

I n the past 40 years no British Prime Minister has shown as much interest in Africa as Tony Blair. He was only a child in 1959 when Harold Macmillan made a west, east and south visit to this continent blazing the 'wind of change' message.

Both the British Prime Minister and his Minister of Finance, Gordon Brown, have recently visited Africa, though they have by-passed Malawi. They have been preparing themselves for the role they will play when Britain assumes the presidency of the European Union and the G8 club of rich countries later this year. We understand that when the G8 countries hold their summit in Britain, on top of the agenda will be Africa.

The great Dr James Kwegyir Aggrey used to say Africa is a question. I am not sure whether he was merely referring to the shape of the continent on a world map or if he had something extra in mind. A few questions can indeed be asked about Africa. How is it that the continent, blessed with abundant natural resources, is far poorer than other continents? It is said that in certain African countries standards of living are now lower than they were at the time those countries gained independence. Where the people have been foolish enough to engage in civil wars the reasons for economic decline are easy to see. But many African countries have known years of peace and political stability.

Africa must be rescued from poverty. There is no happiness in poverty. Where there is poverty there is hunger, disease and ignorance. To remain a beggar nation 40 years or more is more a source of shame than of pity. Why can Africans, including Malawians, not do better than they are doing?

Getting assistance from countries that are better off is not shameful. Europeans after the destructive World War II got a good deal of help from the United States of America under the Marshall Plan. Some people are hoping that the G8 and the EU will put up something similar for Africa; a Marshall Plan of sorts.

What we must not forget is that the times in which the Marshall Plan operated were different from present times. The US was giving aid to a continent that was ready to make the best use of it. It is true that some of Europe's highly skilled and educated men and women had been killed during the war.

But many more had survived the Armageddon. The physical capital (buildings, railways and machines) had been destroyed, but the human capital, comprising entrepreneurs, managers and scientists was available to make proper use of the American aid when it came in the form of the Marshall Plan.

At the time the Americans were providing aid to the mother countries of their founding fathers, the Cold War was replacing the blitzkrieg. America and the then Soviet Union, who were once allies against Nazi Germany, were now in competition to convert other countries to their economic and political systems.

During the time of rivalry between the superstates, some countries in the third world, which was made up of developing countries, were able to obtain the aid they needed simply by being pro-America and against the Soviet Union.

The days of the Cold War are over. The donors are prescribing tough terms on which they give loans and grants. Those needy countries that fulfil the conditions receive sympathetic responses; those which do not are left out in the cold.

This means that whatever the G8 club and the EU will agree about the developing countries during the presidency of the British delegation it will not automatically be available to us. We shall have to meet the conditions.

The current political and economic situation in Malawi is a cause for anxiety. Political factions in Africa often end up in feuds. Hence, vocal factions are not a healthy development of democracy. The sooner the president of the UDF and the State President patch up their differences the better for the nation as a whole. I understand they do not want a *mlamulankunzi* (a peace-broker between bulls), as the Zulus say. But most fellow citizens I have talked to remember an adage that says whatever happens here will affect us all.

A tense political atmosphere is not good for Malawi. Investors do not go to countries with an uncertain future. Some months back I put forward the view that President Mutharika should concentrate on bringing his administration up to the necessary standards and spend less time on the misdeeds of the previous regime. I feared that dwelling too much on the misdeeds of the past generates antagonists. And this is what has in fact happened.

There was a cacophony of disapproval in opposition political circles when it was learned that the President would spend a few days holiday in Singapore en route home from Taiwan. I was much less concerned with the stopover as I thought the President would have the chance to visit another of the Tigers of the Far East and perhaps chat with someone there on transforming a country within a generation from third to first world status. Have you read the biography of Lee Kuan Yew? There is so much in it to learn.

Whatever those in Malawi cherish about privatisation they must not assume that by itself it is an open sesame to accelerated economic development. How much privatisation was there in the countries of the Far East when they were achieving impressive economic growth rates? Not 1 per cent.

Privatising State enterprises in less developed countries like Malawi is not the same thing as privatising State enterprises in Europe or America. Overseas privatisation is taking place within already industrialised and diversified economies. We are at the beginning. A large part of Malawi's economy has yet to be monetised. Homegrown entrepreneurs are still in short supply. More firms must start from scratch.

The State still has a duty to set up enterprises where private entrepreneurs fear to go. When the State has sold one forestry plantation it should open another. The State has to be entrepreneurial. That is the message from the Far East.

The money received from the sale of privatised firms should be reinvested in wealth-generating activities instead of being used as handouts for the sake of winning short-term popularity. There should be a gradual phasing out of free fertiliser. People should be reminded of the Biblical injunction that they should get their bread from the sweat of their brow. It is better to give people the opportunity to work than to give them the dole.

10 May 2005

WHAT IS MALAWI'S PHILOSOPHY OF EDUCATION?

E ducation has been described broadly to mean any situation where one person imparts knowledge to another. In this essay we shall confine the term education to what goes on in our schools.

Education in the broader sense has been around for as long as mankind has existed as *Homo sapiens*. Education in the sense of what is taught in schools was introduced into this country by missionaries from Scotland during the last quarter of the 19th century.

The missionaries had clear aims for the education they introduced. They taught Africans to read and write in their own languages so that they could read the Bible and sing hymns. The more progressive of the missionaries went on to teach Africans English, and skills such as carpentry, masonry and elements of medicine, to enable them to find employment as clerks and vocational assistants. These missionaries appreciated the fact that, as Benjamin Franklin said: "It is difficult for an empty bag to stand upright." If it is true that man cannot live by bread alone, it is equally true that he cannot survive on religious doctrine alone.

The American educationalist John Dewey (1859–1952) said that education as such has no aims, and that it is the people involved who have aims. There are other philosophers of education who say education, apart from the teachers and students, has its own aims. Be this as it may, what are the aims of those who build schools in Malawi?

Basically there are three aims of education and of those engaged in education. The first is to impart knowledge and understanding, because these are the essential values of civilised mankind. A society made up of people who are acquainted with science, technology and art is better equipped to survive in this world than a society lacking these things.

Secondly, education must be given to a person whilst he is still young to prepare him for self-support, survival and prosperity in the future. Education imparts knowledge and knowledge is power. A knowledgeable person is not a slave of superstition. Professor Gary Becker, a Nobel Prizewinner in Economics,

Biographies

has often pointed out that in the labour market, high-school dropouts and high-school graduates are paid differently. The better educated earn more than the less educated. The more education we give to our children the better the chance they will have in the future to get well-paying jobs.

The third aim of education is to serve society, especially the nation. Writing in 1926 on *The Aims of Education*, Britain's most erudite philosopher of the 20th century, Bertrand Russell, had this to say about Chinese education: "It produced stability and art, it failed to produce progress or science. The traditional education of the Chinese is not suited to the modern world and has been abandoned by the Chinese themselves. Modern Japan affords the clearest indication of the tendency which is prominent among all the Great Powers, the tendency to make national greatness the supreme purpose of education. The aim of Japanese education is to produce citizens who shall be devoted to the State through the training of their passions, and useful to it through the knowledge they have acquired."

Somewhere in his autobiography Charles de Gaulle, France's World War II hero and post-war President, says that France's ideal is greatness, or words to that effect. At the end of the last Great War, the French introduced into their educational system a school that trained an élite of administrators who became the envy of the world and which was responsible for restoring France's place among the comity of nations.

The time has come when we should articulate our aims of education. We cannot be sure our educational system is effective unless first we make clear to ourselves its objectives.

For the individual, education should aim at improving his or her mind. He must understand the environment, so that in whatever he does he is not a slave of ignorance and unworthy passions. Some people say ignorance is bliss. Others do not.

God created man to evolve intellectually and mentally, not to live by instinct alone. To master the environment, our education system must produce persons who constantly ask: "Why are things like this, and how can I make them better?" The education system, in other words, must produce the individual who believes in making contributions to the progress of science and art. The individual must be a non-conformist up to a point. The great civilisations of the world were the result of an élite of innovators: Socrates, Plato, Aristotle, Isaac Newton, Thomas Edison, Henry Ford – the list is endless.

In order to prepare our students for the life of invention and innovation we must encourage the reading of biographies in schools and training colleges.

When they study electricity, let them read the biography of Thomas Edison. When they study how to repair a radio let them read about Marconi. When they study literature they must find out how the author wrote his or her classic.

The aim should be to encourage the student to be an originator of ideas, not a mere imitator. HIV/Aids and endemic famines are destroying Africa, but how many Africans are working 24 hours a day doing research that might overcome these plagues?

Secondly, education must enable the individual to gain employment both at home and abroad. Greek and Latin have their uses in training the mind but they do not interest employers looking for competent managers and technicians. Our students must master their mother languages and those international languages which are a repository of modern discoveries. English, German, French, Russian, Japanese and Chinese deserve special attention.

As a nation what would we like to be? A military power? No. We should like to be a nation that enjoys high living standards. The Nordic countries testify to the fact that you can be small and yet prosperous and happy. Switzerland is a worthy role model for Malawi, as is Taiwan, which has managed to succeed economically and now generously assists struggling countries such as Malawi.

Our educational system must aim at making Malawi successful in international markets for products and services. Products are made at home, costs are recovered and profits are made in export markets. It must produce managers and engineers of international calibre.

13 May 2005

AN ECONOMIC SYSTEM
FOR NATIONAL GOALS

Most of the African countries south of the Sahara have been independent since the 1960s. This is long enough a duration in which the continent could have hatched its own economic and political philosophers. Alas, there have been no leaders of thought either in economic or political spheres; at least, not of continental influence.

With the failure of African socialism no one has suggested anything else in its place. Burdened with international debts and mass poverty, most African presidents have opted to pursue economic policies dictated by donors and international finance institutions. But almost everywhere that these policies have been tried, success has been minimal. Africa has still to discover an economic policy of its own to reach the brave new world of prosperity.

This policy must clarify the roles of the State and the private sector. The problem is to determine where one role ends and the other begins. John Maynard Keynes said: "The most important agenda of the State relates not to those activities that private individuals are fulfilling but to those functions which fall outside the sphere of the individual, to those decisions which are made by no one if the State does not make them."

There is much in this for the guidance of policy makers both in developed and developing countries. The role of the State in the two economic categories is bound to be different. Most of the things being done by private individuals in developed countries are not being done by anyone in developing countries. In a developing country like Malawi, therefore, the State must either do those things that are not being done or urge and assist private individuals and bodies corporate to do them.

It is taken for granted that the role of the State is to develop the physical and social infrastructures. There must be roads and bridges, utilities such as electricity and water, minimum social services such as health, education, security and defence.

With these infrastructures in place, it is hoped that a country could attract investment both at home and from other countries. In the past ten years there has been little Foreign Direct Investment (FDI). Malawi does not possess rare natural resources such as oil or diamonds; what she has, her neighbours also have.

Faced with a situation even more hopeless and hostile than ours, Mr Lee Kuan Yew, first Prime Minister of Singapore, tells us: "We had to create a new kind of economy, try new methods; we had to make extraordinary efforts to become a tightly knit, rugged and adaptable people who could do things better and cheaper than our neighbours."

To be able to attract FDI to Malawi there must be something super-attractive. If we remain average in everything we shall never be noticed. In the present global economy, potential investors are choosers, not mere takers of what is offered.

Economic equity is one of the major goals of a democratic society. There should be equality of opportunity for all citizens regardless of colour, tribe, gender or religion. It is the duty of the State to put in place legislation outlawing any form of discrimination. Nay, it must, in certain cases, empower the weaker members of society so that they can hold their own in the race for self-improvement.

Says Lee Kuan Yew: "We cannot afford to forget that public order, personal security, economic and social progress plus prosperity are not the natural order of things, that they depend on ceaseless effort and attention from an honest and effective government that the people elect."

Currently in Malawi the question whether we shall have an effective government up to the next general election depends not only on the qualities of leadership in the governing party but also on the opposition.

Whilst economic security in developed countries means having a steady job and receiving unemployment benefits, in Malawi it means having enough food at the household level throughout the year. Here, cooperation between the State and the individual is obviously desirable. But it seems that neither the State nor the individual is doing the right things to achieve perpetual food security. We have at times achieved food self-security, as when Aleke Banda was Minister of Agriculture for the first time. Since then, we have not quite achieved that kind of success. Apparently we have not established a formula for success.

In *The Nation* of 9 May 2005, a successful farmer in Lilongwe, Patrick Gaven, is quoted as saying: "There are a lot of people who can produce enough food for their own consumption, but they do not want to work and work hard because they know the Government is going to help them with free food."

Unfortunately, this is too true. The dependency spirit hovers over the whole country. Every head of household must be told that it is his/her primary responsibility to see that the family does not starve by working extra hard and by being frugal with what he has harvested.

From the time the *Beveridge Report* was issued at the end of World War II in Britain, and in other developed countries, achieving full employment has been one of the major economic goals. I have been following British public affairs keenly for the best part of half a century. There have been business cycles where unemployment has risen too high. In the time of Prime Ministers Heath and Wilson, Britain was being dubbed 'the sick man of Europe'. Now she is the robust man of Europe, thanks first to Dame Margaret Thatcher and, secondly, to Tony Blair's wisdom in turning his back on left-wing socialism and adopting policies that ensure economic growth without which full employment and poverty alleviation become a mirage.

In the context of our country, what has liberalisation achieved in terms of employment? Advocates of free enterprise say that it ensures incompetent businesses fail and that efficient ones blossom. This is fine if the failed and successful are both domestic businesses. In this case people who lose jobs in the bankrupt firm may find alternative employment in the emerging ones. But if the domestic firm is driven out of business by foreign imports, unemployment is aggravated without any compensation elsewhere in the domestic economy. It is in the foreign country that employment is generated. The management of Nzeru Radio Company and others that are facing cut-throat competition from abroad ought to be given a hearing.

When the American steel industry found itself hard-pressed by European steel in the US market, President George W. Bush put up tariffs and invited the European Union to enter into fresh negotiations. For some years the American Government has been asking the Chinese Government to revalue its currency. Chinese goods are undercutting American products in America, throwing many people out of employment. America does not want this situation to continue.

Whilst it is true that if Malawian people manufactured goods of high quality they would hold their own in world markets, products of poor workmanship from overseas are flooding the Malawi market, creating unemployment.

LEADERSHIP IN BUSINESS

R ecently, students of Business Management at the Polytechnic invited me to give a talk on why the Malawi economy is not growing fast enough and what can be done to accelerate development. I had to begin by saying that giving just one answer would be presumptuous. It was better to analyse each sector of the economy from primary to tertiary to see just why the pace was slow there.

Visible symbols of economic development and growth are successes at the level of individual firms. If more businesses in a given year realise profits, expand and employ more people this is reflected in the health of the economy. If too many firms go bankrupt and lay off workers, that is evidence of poor performance in the economy as a whole.

In Malawi, for at least a decade, we have witnessed companies that were once household names disappear. One has in mind Brown and Clapperton and Kandodo whilst others such as David Whitehead and Sons had to be rescued from the precipice. Finding the secret to corporate success may offer a key to what is right or wrong about the economy as a whole.

When a national team wins an international match, who is responsible for the success: the captain, the coach or the players themselves? What about when the team loses; who should be blamed? When the army is defeated on the battlefield, who is at fault – the general or the private soldiers?

In most cases the football captain will criticise the coach or the players whilst the latter will criticise the captain. Similarly, the general will condemn the private soldiers for being cowardly, whilst the soldiers will criticise the general for equipping them poorly or giving commands at the wrong time.

Genuine and honest leadership never quibbles when things go wrong. Former President of the United States Harry Truman placed a plaque on his desk that read: "The buck stops here." Rudolph W. Giuliani, former mayor of New York, says in his autobiography, *Leadership*, that he used to put a sign on his desk saying: "I'm responsible."

There is an outcry in the business community about unfair competition from abroad. Some business leaders are saying that the government through its liberalisation policies has exposed local manufacturers to the unfair practices of foreign competitors. This could be an accurate explanation of why our firms are not performing better. But the reasons could also be found in the quality of our business leaders.

Who are the business leaders? People known variously as managing directors, executive secretaries, chief executives, company presidents and boards of directors are familiar examples. What does it take to be a successful business leader or to be an effective chief executive?

In the history of individual firms we come across a variety of persons who have made a success of their profession as chief executives. Some have been well educated, with degrees in business management, finance, engineering or the humanities. Others have not gone beyond the high-school diploma and yet have been successful. Some have had imposing statures whilst others have been less impressively endowed. Most have been men, but some have been women. What common traits do such people share that enable them to achieve the same goals?

Though whilst they were holding lower management positions they were specialists, as CEOs they are very good as generalists. They acquaint themselves with every aspect of the business – finance, marketing, production and so on. This enables them to judge the performance of divisional heads.

They work very hard. They are involved in business activities for at least 16 hours a day, 7 days a week. They rarely go on vacation and even when they do, their minds are on the business.

They see as their mission success in business. When they take an interest in public affairs, the aim is to further their business interests. Cost control and profit maximisation is the passion of their life.

In the decade or two preceding this century, in the United States, one of the best-known and respected chief executives was Lee Iacocca of the Ford and Chrysler Motor Companies. In his autobiography he said: "In the end, all business operations can be reduced to three words; people, product and profits. People come first. Unless you've got a good team, you can't do much with the other two."

All successful chief executives are meticulous at selecting key members of staff, such as departmental and divisional managers. Second-rate chief executives prefer to be surrounded by mediocre personalities, friends, lovers and such others. These people do not appoint those who appear cleverer than themselves in case they supplant them.

Truly great chief executives do the opposite. They do not appoint men or women with the same weaknesses as themselves, but those who can complement them. They treat such selected personnel with fairness. They coach, they inspire their subordinates, but they do not suffer fools gladly. Anyone who cannot be moulded into the culture of the business is fired at once.

Jack Welch, the legendary former CEO of General Electric USA, had this to say to a *Newsweek* reporter: "The team with the best players usually does win. And that is why, very simply, you need to invest the vast majority of your time and energy as a leader in three activities. First, you must have the right people. Second, you must guide, critique and help them. And finally, you must build confidence in them and encourage them to achieve beyond their dreams."

Top-class chief executives plan their work and work their plan. They jealously guard their daily schedules. They do things according to their priorities, not according to those of someone else. They are strict with time and do not welcome people who just barge in for a chat.

Top class executives are not risk averse, but neither are they foolhardy in making investments. John H. Johnson, multi-millionaire proprietor of *Ebony* magazine, wrote in his autobiography: "I started, as usual, small. A small step gives you the courage to make a bigger step. And a big step gives you the courage to run."

Most great executives are not satisfied with yesterday's success. They do not rest on their laurels. They constantly seek ways to produce better goods at lower cost.

Says Bill Gates: "Our success is based on only one thing; good products. It's not very complicated." He dropped out of the Harvard University Law School at the age of 19 to pursue his interest in computer technology and then co-founded the Microsoft Corporation. Now Gates is reputed to be the richest man in the United States.

PRAISING MISSIONARIES, CRITICISING MPS

During the Gorodi Road centenary celebrations at Livingstonia, President Bingu wa Mutharika is reported to have asked: "If these missionaries were able to fend for themselves, why can't Malawians do the same?"

This was a pertinent question to ask. During colonial days Nyasas (Malawians) were respected and envied by fellow Africans and given preferential treatment by European employers.

Among the African community of nations today, I doubt if there is anything outstanding about Malawians that other people would wish to emulate. There is a good deal of potential about us, but much less is being achieved. You can realise you are a failure by observing what others are doing and achieving.

There are many things to feel modest about in Malawi. Everyone is saying our education system has declined in quality; students, teachers and invigilators resort to cheating at examinations. Our soccer has yet to produce successors to the likes of Kinnah Phiri. Our politics is just disgusting; our MPs are so greedy for power that they do not mind ignoring the Constitution and the rule of law. These are but some of our shortcomings; the list is not exhausted.

We are a nation burdened by failure. How can we attain success in our endeavours? By exploring the methods and history of missionaries in this country, we may gain an insight into what it takes to succeed in any endeavour.

The first Christian missionaries came to this country in July 1861. They were members of the Universities Mission to Central Africa (UMCA), a society of the Church of England. They started work at Magomero in Chiradzulu. Two years later they had to abandon that work and go to Zanzibar.

That mission failed because of lack of policy and because of misfortune. When their leader, Bishop Frederick Mackenzie, saw members of the Yao and Nyanja tribes quarrelling he took sides by supporting the Nyanja. The Yao burned mission shelters. The misfortunes took the form of deaths of missionary after missionary.

In 1875, missionaries arrived from the Free Church of Scotland. They went to Mangochi. They were led by Dr Robert Laws, a medical man. He noticed that though the Nyanja were the majority tribe, the Yao were the rulers of the country. His policy was not to take sides in native quarrels but to act as peacemaker. He continued this policy when he went to the Northern Region of Malawi, where the Ngoni were dominant, and north-eastern Zambia, where the Bemba were feared by everyone.

Though some chiefs begged him to take sides with them, Laws persistently said he had come for peoples of all tribes and that his role was to be a peacemaker rather than a facilitator of victory. He was trusted by all tribes amongst whom he worked. His work flourished long before the advent of British rule in 1891.

Those who are in charge of religious affairs today should learn a lesson from Dr Laws. Their role is to promote peace, friendship and justice, not to be makers or un-makers of presidents. If they go too deep into politics, their spiritual work will suffer.

A good example is attendance at St Michael and All Angels, Blantyre. In years past if you went late to the 10.30 am service you would find all seats filled. But these days when I attend this service I find it with only one quarter of the seats filled. Where have all the people gone who used to fill up every pew? Perhaps they are the ones attending revival sessions of the independent churches elsewhere in town.

Jesus Christ taught us that it is easier to see a speck of dust in someone else's eye than in one's own. Some church leaders are busy preaching about what they think is wrong in politics. They are not doing much to find out what has caused the drop in attendance at their own churches or prayer houses. The early missionaries understood their objectives. They bent their energies to achieving these. A church whose leaders try to do those things which are best left to other experts or professionals will experience a decline in membership.

The secret of success is to concentrate on your calling and not pretend that you can provide solutions to all other peoples' problems. When a religious leader comments on politics, his aim should be to create harmony where there is conflict.

One other lesson the missionaries can teach us is that if you win the confidence and friendship of people you can accomplish major projects even with meagre resources.

Zimbabwean authors of a book entitled *From Iron Age to Independence*, D. E. Needham et al, tell us that at one time, "the Northern Province of Malawi became the most educationally advanced in the whole of Central

Africa". This was in the part of Nyasaland known as the dead north. How did the Livingstonia missionaries do this?

They went into the villages and learned the languages spoken there; Tumbuka, Tonga, Ngonde and Ngoni, and convinced the people that Christian education – both academic and vocational – was good for them. The missionaries offered teachers.

In return the people offered the teachers accommodation and food. As a result, with little financial expenditure, much was achieved. When Laws sent a report of the progress to his sponsors in Scotland they expressed surprise and disbelief. How could he have built so many schools and prayer houses on so small a budget?

Whoever wants to know if it is still possible to organise the energies of the people for self-help should read the autobiography of Reverend Father Stephen Carr, *Surprised by Laughter*. Carr is a Church Missionary Society missionary (Anglican) who served in southern Sudan, Uganda and Nigeria before coming to this country in 1989. He and his wife forsook the comforts of western civilisation and dwelt among the southern Sudanese in grass-thatched houses.

He says: "A great leader can get much work done provided he or she wins the confidence of the people for whom the projects are intended. You cannot win the confidence of the people by offending donors who feed them during hard times."

One other lesson the missionaries teach us is that greatness is not to be measured by the position you hold in life, but by the success you achieve in any position.

What position did Mother Theresa of India hold in the Roman Catholic hierarchy, and what position did Dr Albert Schweitzer hold in his Protestant church? They are remembered by their deeds.

22 November 2005

BETWEEN MALAWI, SCOTLAND

Contacts between the people of Malawi and those of Scotland started in 1856 when Dr David Livingstone arrived in the Lower Shire with 27 carriers of the Kololo or Makololo tribe from Barotseland (Zambia). Livingstone died in Zambia in 1873. In 1874 patriotic Scots met in Glasgow and Edinburgh and resolved to go to that part of Africa Livingstone had recommended for missionary effort and establish missions in the name of his birthplace, Blantyre, and in his own name. Subscriptions were handed in by people of various denominations.

Towards the end of 1875 Dr Robert Laws of the Free Church of Scotland arrived in Mangochi at the court of Chief Mponda, a Muslim. Laws had the knack of befriending tribal rulers who usually had bad reputations abroad.

Yao chiefs such as Mponda were reputed to be agents of Arab and Swahili slave traders and unlikely to welcome Christian missionaries. But Mponda received Laws genially and allowed him to set up an experimental station at Cape Maclear.

In 1876 Henry Henderson, with help from Dr Laws, obtained permission from Chief Kapeni, also a Yao and a Muslim, to start a mission settlement of the Church of Scotland between Soche, Ndirande and Nyambadwe mountains. This settlement was named Blantyre Mission and was the nucleus of the now sprawling city of Blantyre.

In 1878 those people of Scotland who had financed the Livingstonia Mission launched a commercial company that later became known as the African Lakes Company, but to the ordinary African it was known as Mandala.

This company was to be one of the tools for combating the slave trade, of which Dr Livingstone had been an inveterate enemy. He had said over and over again that "if you introduce honest trade in Africa, Africans will be diverted away from the slave trade". Christianity and commerce were to be introduced as weapons against man's inhumanity to man.

The African Lakes Company started operating halfway between the River Mudi and what is now Queen Elizabeth Central Hospital in 1878 under the joint management of two sons of an Edinburgh doctor; John and Frederick Moir. Whenever Laws visited a chief he took Frederick with him. He would say to the chief: "I am here to bring the message of Jesus Christ to your people, to teach them to read and write and also skills to make things that we make. My colleague is here to trade with you if you are interested."

Scottish missionaries put equal emphasis on spiritual and secular education. Every missionary was required to learn the local African language. Within a few years the missionaries were able to preach in the vernacular. They were possibly the first to put Malawian languages into written form. Men like Dr Alexander Hetherwick of Blantyre Mission wrote an English-Chinyanja dictionary whilst Dr William Turner of Livingstonia wrote English-Chitumbuka and Tonga dictionaries. They translated the Bible and church hymnary into widely spoken languages such as Chinyanja and Chitumbuka. They also encouraged Africans to compose their own hymns.

G. M. Trevelyan, author of the monumental *History of England* and several other works on English socio-economic history, says that standards of education in 18th century Scotland were higher than in England. Scots brought with them to Malawi these high standards in primary and vocational teaching.

Stephen Neill, a former professor of theology at the universities of Nairobi and Hamburg, says in his book *A History of Christian Missions*: "Nyasaland was divided between the UMCA and the Scots – the two great Presbyterian churches of Scotland coming in with a wonderful array of enterprise; evangelistic, medical, educational, industrial and agricultural, and certainly amongst the best organised mission projects in the world."

By the beginning of the 20th century Nyasaland was one of the most literate of British African colonies. Lacking opportunities for employment at home, a large proportion of these educated Malawians went to the Rhodesias, now Zambia and Zimbabwe, and to South Africa to work as clerks, artisans and teachers. They were highly prized by European employers there. They often called themselves Black Scots.

The thorough primary education and the system of church administration to which they were exposed prepared students of the Blantyre and Livingstonia missions for leadership. Some were made members of Kirk Sessions where their views were sought on the way the church should be administered. These men and women were made to feel that they were responsible and educated enough to be consulted on matters that affected their lives.

In secular matters they were the first to seek recognition from government.

They led in founding the district native associations that presented African grievances to Government. These early pioneers included men such as John Grey Kufa, James Matinga and Charles Mlanga in the South, and Levi Mumba, Charles Chinula and Yesaya Zerenje Mwase in the North.

Towering above these were Dr Hastings Banda, founder of the Malawi nation, and Clements Kadalie of South African fame. They were alumni of Livingstonia. John Chilembwe and James Sangala were products of the Blantyre mission.

In 1884 the German Chancellor, Otto von Bismarck, invited European nations interested in Africa to a conference in Berlin. They agreed to peacefully partition Africa on the basis of each country's existing sphere of influence. If you look again at the map of East Central Africa you will notice that Malawi is a much smaller country than its neighbours. This had nothing to do with the weaknesses or strengths of Africans residing in these parts of Africa. The existence of modern Malawi owes its origin to the Scottish missionary and commercial institutions already introduced by 1884.

The British Prime Minister at the time, Lord Salisbury, showed no particular interest in claiming this part of Africa for Britain. When the Portuguese claimed the Shire Highlands to be part of Mozambique Salisbury was willing to let them have the Highlands up to Lake Malawi. Those were the days when a quarter of the earth was flying the Union Jack. Britain had India, South Africa, Nigeria, Canada and many others. Giving way on the Shire Highlands was not seen as a big loss.

Hetherwick and David Clement Scott of Blantyre mission and John Moir of African Lakes Company did not want to operate under Portuguese rule. They appealed to their sponsors at home to take up the matter with Lord Salisbury. Thousands of leading men and women in Edinburgh and elsewhere signed a petition demanding that Britain should protect its nationals and the Africans amongst whom they were working. In May 1891 this country became a British Protectorate.

THE SEAMY SIDE OF OUR CULTURE

I t is generally pleasant to think of our culture in positive terms. For example, that despite the prevailing poverty we are a happy people and most of us are God-fearing. But cruel and sordid activities are regularly and often being reported by the media. Some of the cruel things being done require a multi-faceted approach to their elimination. Revision of the statutes may not be the only solution.

A few years ago, someone committed a series of outrages on women in Chiradzulu, removing their private parts. Despite the deployment of policemen, it took some time before a suspect was arrested and taken to court. Several of those arrested with him were acquitted.

Equally gruesome was the story of a pregnant woman who was skinned alive and her baby removed. This was a woman's cruelty to a fellow woman. If there was a well-organised adoption system perhaps acts like these, including the theft of babies, might not be so common.

The cruelest are those acts linked to superstition and magic. The lust for money is the root of all evil. Those who mutilate other people's bodies, or exhume dead bodies, use the human organs in the concoction of their witchcraft and magic. They believe this magic will make them rich.

Superstitions about easy ways to make money exist in every society. I remember from my schooldays our teacher from Kirkcaldy, Scotland, telling us that when she was a girl she and her friends used to go into the hills searching for a five-leafed clover. They believed that if found it would make them rich.

One of the novels I loved reading in the past was called *The Black Tulip*. One day I asked our Bonn embassy driver, a Dutchman, what was the significance of the black tulip. In the novel it was made a source of conflict. He told me that in his country some people believe that if you come across a black tulip you will become rich.

Such superstitions are harmless. But the ones among us which involve murder or dismemberment are horrendous. The lawyer and the social psychologist should join hands and see that ritual murders are eradicated. The lawyer should update the law.

When the British established a protectorate over this country in 1891, one of their first acts was to outlaw *mwabvi* – witch screening by the use of poisonous tree bark. They did not recognise the existence of witchcraft and therefore they would not entertain accusations of witchcraft in their courts.

Superstition and witchcraft are twin brothers. During colonial days the Colonial Office and British universities used to send out anthropologists to study our cultures and social habits. Our rulers wanted to understand us better. Now we need to understand ourselves.

There are some members of our society who seem to live in a world of their own. They are doing things reminiscent of the darkest days of African history, when people would sell their relatives, or even children, to the slave traders.

Amongst educated people, deception and corruption have become rampant. Instead of working hard for examination success, some students prefer to spend time learning how to forge education certificates. Some have obtained jobs or entered university using false documents. Some Immigration office staff have been bribed to issue false passports to foreigners. Top civil servants are being revealed by auditors to have mishandled public funds entrusted to them. Yet all these people are earning regular salaries. They fail to resist avarice and covetousness.

Our tastes for worldly goods are now very sophisticated. We love the products of Western science and technology. But we are slow to imitate the inventions and innovations that make them possible. No wonder Africa continues to trail behind other continents.

We admire a person who spends lavishly – even when the money is not his – rather than the person who lives a frugal life. No wonder we remain poor even after occupying well-paid positions.

Organisations such as the Nyasaland African Congress and the Malawi Congress Party were first financed by contributions from their members. As we approached independence, sympathisers from abroad started to donate generously. As time went on people starting new organisations began to depend almost exclusively on these grants from donors. If the funding stopped, then so did the existence of the organisation. The spirit of self-help that our fathers and grandfathers had in abundance is not much in evidence now.

Superstition makes people behave worse than wild beasts. We hear of female witches teaching their witchcraft to children whilst men rape the children. It is difficult to understand these people. Normally witchcraft is practised in secret and only with fellow adults. To be known as a witch or a wizard is to risk being ostracised or killed.

What satisfaction does a man get from raping a child? None, certainly, but he believes that the act will add extra potency to his magic concoctions.

Darkness is on the rise. Light is receding. Cry the beloved country.

3 February 2006

OBJECTIVES OF RURAL DEVELOPMENT

What does the term 'rural development' mean to most of us? I believe it simply means increasing agricultural production. But it also means more. Industries and services can be located in rural areas to supplement purely agricultural development.

With the advent of Western contacts, especially from the time this country became a British protectorate in 1891, development and urbanisation have meant the same thing. If development involved little urbanisation, it was said to be non-development. Hence, because little urbanisation was taking place in the Northern Region – though schools were spread widely – that part of the country was said to be 'dead'.

Rural development has to have a multi-faceted approach because rural people today, as with those in urban areas, have tastes for many things, not just food alone. Foreign styles and tastes which influence people in urban centres move on to influence people in rural areas.

Objectives for rural development ought to be spelt out before projects are launched. Without clear objectives we cannot be sure we are making progress. The following are, or ought to be, the objectives of developing the rural hinterland.

First, there should be enough food production so that the people live off the harvest from their gardens or farms. It is pathetic that most people in villages should be going to market to buy maize instead of selling it. A farmer is a person who produces food for his own consumption, and for sale. We do not expect him to be a buyer of staple foods – maize, beans and groundnuts.

Secondly, farmers should produce enough food for sale in urban centres. People in towns do not grow crops, but make things that generally are not made in rural areas. The two parts of the land then exchange what is surplus to their needs.

Thirdly, rural centres should produce cash crops that can be sold both in domestic and foreign markets. Even maize can serve as a cash crop when there are famines in other countries. It is not only Malawi that experiences periodic food shortages. Every opportunity should be made to produce for foreign markets in order to earn foreign exchange.

And fourthly, the rural centres should be developed so as to encourage people to remain there, and those who have nothing to do in urban centres to go back and make a living there.

Life in towns gives a false impression of it being easy to become rich. The truth is that the apparently higher wages people earn in towns are easily taken away by higher rents, food prices and by the temptation to buy what others are buying.

Visit townships such as Ndirande and be shocked by what you see there. There is congestion of houses and stench and filth everywhere. There is so much noise around. You see children playing in muddy pools of water. You wonder that only some of these people get sick, since all of them are exposed to pathogens. Certainly, village life is much healthier. Rural life should be enhanced to encourage people to stay there.

Rains have now come, but with mixed blessings. Adequate moisture for the land has been followed by flash floods that have driven people from their homes, especially in the Lower Shire. This is not the first time we have been visited by torrential rains, but we do not seem to learn long-lasting lessons.

It has been said that if you are given a lemon, make lemonade from it. A lemon is bitter, lemonade is sweet. The flash floods are destructive, but if they are trapped in reservoirs they could be used for irrigation and even, perhaps, the generation of electricity. To be civilised is to have the ability to harness natural forces to man's advantage. Why are we apparently helpless whenever heavy rains arrive?

It is possible, the experts say, that at the end of this rainy season there will be a bumper harvest. If so, this will not be the first time. In the year that the starter pack scheme was introduced there was such a surplus that we were able to export part of it. That bumper harvest, however, was followed by an acute shortage of the staple food, maize. We had learned nothing from Joseph of Egypt in the days of the Pharaohs. In the seven years that there were plentiful yields, Joseph stored the excess. In the lean years, with the stored harvest Egypt was able not only to feed its own people, but also those from other countries such as Joseph's father and brothers.

Progress is made whenever people learn from their failures as well as from their successes. We should analyse the causes of the great famines which have visited this country from time to time. We should also try to understand why, during other times, we have managed to realise a good harvest. For continued success we should avoid those mistakes which led to crop failure and repeat things which resulted in bumper harvests and which might do the same this year.

One reason why this year we might have a good harvest is that there is adequate moisture in the soil. This moisture has been provided by the rains. We know from past experience that we cannot rely on the winds to bring us good rains every year. This is the reason we must take seriously agriculture by irrigation. We understand that it was because the monsoon rains were supplemented by irrigation in South-East Asia that the countries there experienced their 'green revolutions'. What are we doing just now to channel the torrents into places where the accumulated water can be used in the dry season?

The timely provision of fertilisers will count as one of the elements in the achievement of a good harvest in 2006. We must ensure that for the next rainy season, farmers will be supplied with fertilisers on time. The crops too must be protected from disease and pests. Farmers and producers of chemicals must be in good touch. What about the kind of implements we use? The *jembe* or *khasu* (hoe) is no longer an efficient tool. Our mechanical engineers should try to invent an up-to-date implement that small farmers can use.

No matter how much money a person earns, he will always experience financial hardships if he spends his earnings thoughtlessly. Similarly, no matter how big the *nkhokwes* (maize stores) people have, they will experience hunger if they are wasteful. Well stocked *nkhokwes* plus care taken to protect the cereals from rodents and profligate usage will ensure that there is always enough food for everyone.

24 February 2006

WHAT IS WRONG WITH AFRICAN ECONOMICS?

W e are told *ad nauseam* that Africa has all those bad elements that make life absolute misery for so many of its peoples: perpetual famines, civil wars, corruption, slow pace of development, HIV/Aids and, in some cases, economic decline.

The Africa to which these evils are attributed is that south of the Sahara. Until 1956 nearly all the countries in this region were European colonies. Exceptions were Liberia, Ethiopia and South Africa. The last mentioned had limited democracy which excluded the majority of its people from participation in elections, but otherwise it had its own flag, national anthem and other symbols of independence.

By 1960, many African colonies had regained independence, particularly the French-speaking ones. Tanzania gained independence in 1961, Uganda in 1962, Kenya in 1963 and Malawi and Zambia in 1964. All these countries were well-endowed with natural resources.

In 1965, Singapore, with a small population of 2 million, gained independence – a year after Malawi. With other East Asian countries, it shared characteristic high population densities and an absence of natural resources. It depended on entrepôt business and the presence of the British military for employment. Despite an inauspicious beginning, Singapore now has an annual per capita income of $23,700. This is much higher than even the best-endowed of African countries. It is one of the powerful Tigers of the Far East along with Taiwan, Thailand, Malaysia and South Korea.

Where one country with abundant natural resources fails to develop and its people continue to live in grinding poverty, and where another country, with very scarce natural resources, in two generations moves from third world to first, the explanation can only be found in the quality of human power or human capital. What sort of people live in that successful country? What is their attitude towards wealth and work?

Only befuddled racists nowadays believe that human races are endowed with different levels of intelligence. The truth is that it is environments and cultures that make some people cleverer than others. If we are to understand why development in the Far East was faster than in Africa, then we must probe the cultures and leaderships in those regions.

In the *Taiwan Journal* of 6 January 2006, President Chen of Taiwan is quoted as saying, "The 'Taiwan consciousness' breaks away from the shackles of historical bondage and political dogma, and is founded upon the 23 million people of Taiwan's own self-recognition, their devotion to the land and their understanding of their shared destiny. Irrespective of whence they came, no one now sees this land as a foreign country, or himself as a sojourner passing through. Taiwan is our home and each of us master of this land."

Common loyalty to the land, feeling that you are one people irrespective of where your ancestors came from is the basis of nation building and economic development. A nation split by 'isms' cannot move ahead economically, culturally or politically.

Some African societies with all the potential for growth and prosperity are torn apart by tribal wars and racial antipathy. Civil wars endure for decades. Some countries have suffered economic decline following the expulsion of hard-working racial minorities such as Asians in Uganda under Idi Amin and white farmers in one SADC country. For our African countries to develop, co-existence between people of different origins must be encouraged.

Singapore was recently featured in a copy of *The Weekly Telegraph*. Prime Minister Lee Hsien Loong and his father, former president Lee Kuan Yew, are quoted as saying: "Here in Singapore we have created something unique and precious. Our people, our ideas, our actions have done this. To avoid being swept along by these changes, we have focused on the values of honest, responsible and effective government with morally upright leaders."

During the four decades that sub-Saharan Africa has been independent, how many of its leaders have established effective governments and how many leaders have been morally upright? If the top leadership of the country is dedicated and honest, the chances are that those immediately below will follow suit. If the top leadership puts the interest of the nation before that of anybody else – including the self – the rest of the population is likely to try to do so. Development has accelerated in those countries where leaders by example have imbued a nation as a whole with the spirit of selflessness and patriotism.

It is very unwise for certain categories of public servants here in Malawi to be demanding salary increases of up to 500% during times when the economy has grown by less than five per cent. A government can raise taxes only according to the growth rate of its economy. You cannot drink water from an empty well. On the other hand, employees will moderate their demands if they see their leaders and the elite living frugal lives. Only a few African leaders tried to do this. I can think of Julius Nyerere of Tanzania and Kenneth Kaunda of Zambia.

Corruption is a vice by no means peculiar to Africa. But in Asia there is the compensating factor that economic growth has taken place despite pockets of corruption. It is illegal to deprive a rich man of his property, but to deprive a poor man of his only goat is a terrible evil. Corruption takes place in African countries that are already poor, thereby making them poorer still.

African leadership and African culture ought to be adjusted so that they act as catalysts to economic development. We have heard often about poverty reduction, poverty elimination and similar phrases. Without cultural reorientation these slogans will remain mere platitudes. We must eliminate from our culture preferences for leisure to labour, consumption to saving, conflict to cooperation and eliminate anything that is negative.

There is a formula for national success just as there is for personal success. For their countries to develop, African leaders must discover and apply the formula for economic success.

14 March 2006

SUGGESTIONS FOR THE MALAWI CONSTITUTION

People decide to live in an association called 'the State', whose executive committee is called 'the Government'. Through the State and its institutions people seek to experience a better life than that which they would have as isolated individuals. Explicitly or implicitly, they have an idea of what good life is. Their communal ideas on this good life constitute their philosophy. This becomes formalised as a Constitution.

Tom Paine, an Englishman, in his book of 1790, *The Rights of Man*, wrote; "The end of all political associations is the preservation of the natural and imprescriptible rights of man – liberty, property, security and resistance of oppression."

In rewriting our Constitution we must study foreign models, but come up with something that is germane to our philosophy of life. Our Constitution must start with our political and economic ideology or doctrine. Having said that, I would like to comment on the difficulties we have experienced in trying to implement the current Constitution.

(a) Separation of powers. Those framing Constitutions have faced the perpetual dilemma of how much power to give to those who have to govern, and how much to withhold from them in case these rulers become tyrants. The doctrine of separation of powers is linked with the French philosopher, Montesquieu. It aims at allocating power to the main branches of government, the Executive, the Legislature and the Judiciary. To allocate all these powers to a single person would be to make that person a terrible tyrant.

No country has managed to live the full logic of separation of powers. The Americans have entrenched into their Constitution 'checks and balances' over the powers of the president and the legislators. Such checks and balances have been misinterpreted by the framers of the Malawi Constitution. To restrain the powers of our President, they made provision for a separately elected Vice-President over whom the President cannot exercise discipline in the way he can over other members of the Cabinet. The Constitution should be revised to give the President the prerogative to select or drop the Vice-President.

In order that a president does not abuse his sovereign powers, he should exercise only those powers that are spelt out in the Constitution, and these powers should be subject to interpretation by the courts. We must avoid two equally bad situations: where a president's powers equal those of a tyrant, and where a president is so weak that he is unable to take charge and the country slides into anarchy.

(b) Parliament. When people speak of checks and balances, they think more of restraining the Executive than Parliament. But the behaviour of members of our National Assembly justifies putting some brakes on this august House. As regards funding, it has been suggested that a budget should be allocated to Parliament which it may then administer as it sees fit. This suggestion should not be readily entertained. From time to time we have seen that although MPs may disagree in the House on such issues as impeachment, they readily agree on suggestions to hike their salaries and allowances, at the expense of the public.

(c) Ministers. These should continue to be Members of Parliament. Should the President drop them from the Cabinet they would continue to be representatives of their constituencies.

(d) Presidential candidates. It has been suggested that our presidents should rotate on a regional basis. This proposal would have the effect of entrenching regionalism into our national politics. Equally undesirable is the proposal to have regional assemblies. Malawi is too small and poor to have duplication of services.

(e) The Senate. It has been proposed that a Senate – a second chamber to the House – be created. This should be postponed indefinitely because its potential usefulness is in doubt. Without doubt are the financial burdens a second chamber would bring upon the country. Those who insist on having the Senate should agree to the trimming of the Lower House to about 150 members, so that the overall expenditure on the Legislature should be no higher than now.

(f) Impeachment of the President. This should be reviewed so that occasions when impeachment is necessary involve the infringement of human rights. Mere failure to observe some laws should be reversed by court procedure. If the President ignores the ruling of the Supreme Court, we can then say he has no respect for the Constitution.

(g) The President's businesses and wealth. I have never heard of Constitutions which stipulate that a president should not have sources of income other than his salary. If this were the case, most able people would be reluctant to contest the presidency. This would be so especially if their immunity from prosecution could be removed by mere court procedure. The withdrawal of presidential immunity should be subject to the concurrence of both the Legislature and the Judiciary.

(h) Rights and duties. Besides laying down the rights of citizens, the Constitution should also provide for duties. Whoever demands rights from the State or society must also observe his duties to it. Even if you did not vote for the elected President, you are obliged to give him due respect because he represents the will of the majority.

(i) Gender issues. What is required is equality between men and women. We know that from ages beyond memory, women have occupied subordinate positions in society, mostly for biological reasons. What is required is to give girls equal opportunity for education so that they can compete equally with boys for any job.

(j) The law should be no stiffer for one gender than for the other. In some judicial systems there is a tendency to punish the husband more severely than the wife for committing the same offence. There should be no inequality before the law.

(k) The death penalty. The abolition of certain laws, such as the death penalty, should be subject to a referendum. No individual has the right to impose his saintliness on the nation. Laws must reflect the philosophy of the people.

(l) Elections. I favour the present 'first past the post' system to continue. It is the simplest to understand. Where a presidential candidate secures less than 50% of the votes, there should be a re-run as has happened in recent years in Ghana and Liberia.

A GLIMPSE INTO MALAWI'S ECONOMIC HISTORY

Theories in economics have been built out of what economists observe in their daily interaction with other people and from studying what happened in the past. A brief review of the economic history of Malawi should enable us to pick out lessons for our present and future economic policy and for our performance.

As everywhere in human history, our first people roamed and lived on whatever they could find in the forest. Then they learned to cultivate crops, to tame livestock and to live a more settled life. Trading arose when Africa came into contact with people from overseas; first came the Arabs and then the Europeans.

The Arabs initially confined their trading to east African coastal settlements. It was their African agents they sent into the interior to buy ivory and slaves. In this way, Indian cloth called sari was introduced and became known as *nsalu* in *Chinyanja* and as *saru* in *Chitumbuka*.

The arrival of the Portuguese on southern and east African coasts had a greater impact on tribal African economies. We are informed that the Portuguese introduced such food crops as maize, cassava, sweet potatoes and several others. We are then made to wonder what our ancestors were eating before these South American products were brought here. Millet and sorghum are mentioned amongst those early foods indigenous to Africa.

Europeans and Africans, from the 16th century onwards, exchanged mostly products of an extractive nature. Europeans bought African slaves and ivory, much to the detriment of local African economies. The British arrived in this country in the mid-19th century. They came to propagate Christianity and to seek raw materials for their factories in Lancashire.

The first British trading business was the African Lakes Company, locally known as Mandala. It obtained tonnes of local materials, not only from Malawi but from as far away as Ujiji in Tanzania. In exchange the company sold Africans cheap Manchester calico and, on occasion, muzzle-loading guns.

Sir Alfred Sharpe and Frederick Lugard, later Lord Lugard, first came here to hunt big game, especially elephants. They were responsible for depleting the elephant population in the country, especially in the Lower Shire Valley. Lugard left eventually to become Governor of Uganda and Nigeria while Sharpe succeeded Harry Johnston here in Malawi as Commissioner and Consul-General.

Missionaries had arrived from Scotland before the country became a British Protectorate. They arrived with guns and ammunition to protect themselves from wild beasts and to provide themselves with meat. But they also did one important thing for the growth of the economy. They brought into the country crops which had not been grown here before. They grew tea and coffee as cash crops, thereby introducing the country to durable international relationships.

The one individual central to the introduction and processing of these cash crops was John Buchanan. He arrived in the country in 1876 and served at the Blantyre Mission as gardener. He was to be dismissed in 1881 for his brutal treatment of African mission servants, but he did great things for the country's agriculture before and after this date.

Before his dismissal he had been posted by the mission to open an outstation in the land of Chief Mlumbe. He settled by the River Mulunguzi. That was to be the beginning of Zomba, the future capital of Nyasaland.

Buchanan spoke both *Chiyao* and *Chinyanja* fluently. He worked closely with Africans whose agriculture practices he respected. He borrowed ideas from them.

He spoke against the sale to Africans of what he called 'fire water', or *kachasu*. Buchanan wrote: "A heavy responsibility rests upon the heads of those who introduce spirits among a race of people who are capable, under proper management and education, of one day becoming a great nation." He wrote these words in 1886. They are a challenge today to those of us who belong to the Malawi nation. Are we ready to make it a great nation? Usually the foundation of greatness is wealth. Our economy is still based on cash crops introduced into the country in the late 19th century.

The growth of economies somewhat resembles the growth of businesses. The concept of product life-cycles is common to both. Malawi's traditional cash crops, such as tea, have reached the plateau stage of their life-cycle. Tobacco, for external reasons, is under great threat. The Malawi economy can be saved through the active introduction of new crops and new industries to start new life-cycles. Soon after World War II, the Colonial Development Corporation (CDC) started a tung estate in the north-east of Mzimba at a small place called Mzuzu. That tung estate blossomed into the city of Mzuzu.

Show me a country that has remained prosperous over a long period and I will show you one that continuously introduces new industries.

16 May 2006

CHINUA ACHEBE
IN AFRICAN LITERATURE

The D.D. Phiri Column mentions the name of Chinua Achebe and it immediately revives in thousands of people the memory of having read his book, *Things Fall Apart.* He wrote other books; *No Longer at Ease, Arrow of God, A Man of the People* and *Anthills of the Savannah.* But it is his first novel, *Things Fall Apart,* published in 1958, that established his name overnight.

When in 1968 Achebe's compatriot Wole Soyinka became the first African to receive the Nobel Prize for Literature, there were many who thought Achebe too should be similarly recognised. Never mind; by 1997 Achebe had received 22 honorary doctorates from universities around the world, including his own country, Nigeria. I have never come across anyone so widely honoured by academic and professional institutions.

Achebe was born in 1930 in the then Eastern Nigeria, an Igbo by tribe. He graduated from Ibadan University and after a spell as a teacher joined the Nigeria Broadcasting Corporation (NBS), rising to the position of director of external broadcasting.

In 1956 whilst with NBS he began working on *Things Fall Apart.* He was wondering how to get his finished manuscript typed when he read an advertisement in the British magazine, *The Spectator,* which offered to type authors' manuscripts at a fee. Achebe sent his work and 22 pounds sterling as requested. On receipt of the fee those in London immediately forgot the manuscript. But, through the help of a friend travelling there, he eventually received a single typed copy. Later, Achebe was heard to say that if the manuscript had been lost he would have been unable to reproduce *Things Fall Apart.*

He sent the typed work to an agent in London where it was rejected by many publishers before it reached the offices of William Heinemann. Here the same doubts were expressed as to whether a novel by an African could appeal to many readers and whether it could be profitable. However, Professor Donald Macrae, with much experience of West Africa and as advisor to Heinemann on educational books, declared it was the best novel he had read since World War II.

Cautiously Heinemann published 2000 copies. It received very good reviews in the British press and was at once awarded the Margaret Wrong Prize. That was the beginning of countless awards to be received by Achebe.

I remember a lecture sponsored by the British Council where the speaker from Britain wondered if Achebe spoke any other language but English. In other words, his English was as good as if it were his mother tongue. It is a hallmark of Achebe's writing that he finds the correct word for anything he wants to say.

At the height of Heinemann's African Writers Series, Achebe's books were earning them a third of their revenue. More than 5 million copies of *Things Fall Apart* had been sold by the end of the 20th century. Achebe was editor of Heinemann's African Writers Series for many years. At the same time he was editing magazines in Nigeria and lecturing at Nsukka University of Nigeria. He was travelling widely.

In 1962, at a Ugandan university, Achebe met a student named James Ngugi who brought him a manuscript titled, *Weep not Child*. Achebe liked the work and advised Heinemann to publish it. That was the beginning of Ngugi's remarkable career as East Africa's most popular writer.

For a great writer, an output of 5 novels is too low. It is true Achebe wrote many poems and short stories, but if he had given more time to the writing of novels he might have produced an even better book than *Things Fall Apart*. I have sometimes been asked to name 'the African novel' that is the standard by which all others are to be judged. I have resisted naming *Things Fall Apart* because I think the great African novel is yet to come.

An American writer, Catherine Drinker Bowen, in her book titled *Biographies,* writes: "If the energy and originality of genius startles people so does the phenomenon of their abundance. Lesser talents produce sparingly, though their production may be exquisite. But true genius produces in shoals, in barrelsful and shelvesful, with the quality rising and falling, as witness Dickens, Thackeray, Tolstoy and Beethoven." Achebe is a talented writer, no doubt, but Africa must continue to wait for its Dickens, Shakespeare and Dumas.

Achebe did not escape controversy. As a lecturer in African literature at Nsukka University he upset admirers of Joseph Conrad when denouncing his *Heart of Darkness* as a racialist literary work. He also reviewed *The Beautiful Ones are not yet Born*, by Ayi Kwei Armah of Ghana, as a sick book, its hero passive and nameless. Armah responded with furious and abusive letters. When the two later met in Nigeria, Armah said to Achebe, "If you found something wrong with my book, why did you not tell me in private?" Armah was justified in taking umbrage. Criticisms from a famous writer can quickly destroy a reputation.

There are two lessons to be learned from the history of *Things Fall Apart*. First, the manuscript was rejected by many publishers. They misjudged it. Do not discard your manuscript because two or three publishers have rejected it. Secondly, some people who handle your manuscript – typists and publishers – may treat your work with indifference and even lose it. You may have taken 5 years writing it but the other fellow does not know that, he or she has their own priorities. It is up to you to keep several copies.

26 May 2006

WHAT ELSE SHALL WE EXPORT?

W e have heard it said that Malawi is to be transformed from an importing to an exporting country, from a consuming to a producing country. These are lofty slogans and they ought to be repeated aloud, because a nation without a vision is already lost.

Following a meeting of the Ghana Investment Advisory Council, President John Kufuor told journalists that 2006 must be the year of "implementation, implementation and implementation" and that mere talk must end.

It takes the joint efforts of the private and public sectors to make an economy move. There must be constant consultation followed by continuous implementation of whatever is agreed upon.

Whenever it is said that Malawi is to be an exporting nation this can only mean that she will export more of that which she is already exporting and that she will start new exports. Malawi exports tea, tobacco, sugar and a few lesser commodities.

In the early 19th century, foreigners such as the Arab popularly known as Jumbe settled at Nkhotakota to buy slaves and ivory. The African Lakes Company, towards the end of the 19th century, undertook what today would be called ivory poaching. These exports involved the extraction of the country's resources without local production or replacement. They merely impoverished the country.

Are we doing the right things to make sure good ideas and slogans bear fruit? How often do representatives of the private and public sectors meet to find out what progress, if any, they are making? What ought to be done must be done today. There is no tomorrow. There is too much talk in politics in this country and most of it is rotten.

Is Malawi to be industrialised through gigantic firms as was the case in South Korea? Or is Malawi to follow the example of Taiwan and make use of small and medium-sized enterprises (SME)? Commentators say that the contribution made by SMEs to economies in Africa are insignificant compared to their contribution to developed economies. There are three possible reasons why SMEs here are not contributing a good deal more.

First, the owners might not be aware of the opportunities that are within their reach. What is it that they can make or manufacture which can be sold, and where? Secondly, they may have the idea of what can be made and sold but be without the technical know-how. There are many watch-repairers in Malawi, but can they also manufacture timepieces? There are many shoe-repairers; why are they not manufacturing and exporting shoes? Many people throughout Africa still go barefoot, so there is potential demand for more shoes.

Thirdly, industries with long gestation periods can be started only by those who have sources of immediate income. Those who have made and saved money in retailing may have the capital to embark on manufacturing businesses. We have commendable examples in Arkay Plastics and in Rab Processors, but we need more. Is there venture capital available in the country? If so, then more publicity should be given to it and to how honest people can access it.

There is much foreign money pouring into the country to teach democracy and human or women's rights. This money is given to NGOs and some of them apparently are not making proper use of it. Their accounts are disputed. The Danes are particularly meticulous about the money they give out. Here in Malawi they have just withdrawn their support from those proved to be non-conforming.

At the same time, we must ask: do we really need foreign money to teach us democracy and human rights? What we do need is much more money to be invested in the production of goods and services as the first step towards the conquest of poverty. The funds which are now being given to NGOs for political and ideological purposes ought to be diverted into venture capital for developing the resources of this country.

Émigré Chinese, both Taiwan and mainland, have contributed to the growth of their countries by way of capital investment and knowledge. When I recently talked to a Malawian visiting here from abroad about this Asian example, he said Malawians who try to come home and relocate find they are not welcome, being seen as competitors. Well, not everyone welcomed Dr Banda when he arrived in 1958, but still he came, saw and conquered.

AFRICAN HISTORY REVISITED

During colonial days African students studied history from books written exclusively by Europeans. This history dwelt on the ancient civilisations of Egypt and Mesopotamia, then Greece and Rome. Very briefly did it allude to the West African kingdoms of Ghana, Mali and Songhai. African students were taught that because tropical Africa had been cut off from North Africa by the Sahara and from Europe by bad harbours, its people had remained backward since the days of Adam and Eve.

This kind of history engendered an African inferiority complex, especially when books written by people such as Arthur Gobineau averred that the black race was genetically inferior to the white.

In 1924, a Ghanaian by the name of Dr James Kwegyir Aggrey, a member of the Phelps-Stokes Commission on African Education, visited most of the sub-Saharan countries. Here in Malawi, at the Henry Henderson Institute on Likoma and in Nkhoma and Livingstonia, Aggrey spoke as he had spoken elsewhere of an eagle that lived amongst chickens. He said the eagle had forgotten its true nature. It was only on being reminded that it was an eagle that it flew up, leaving the chickens on the ground. "We are the eagles," said Aggrey. "Let us stretch forth our wings and fly."

He talked of how he had gone to America and obtained higher education. He advised young Africans to make use of what they had to get what they wanted. Aggrey taught Africans to be proud of their colour and not ashamed of it. They were as good as the people of other races.

Out of Aggrey's philosophy there sprang a new generation of African scholars that went overseas and obtained higher education.

One group, once back home, set about agitating for independence. Another group, in which we are interested here, set about digging into ancient documents to find the truth about the African past. "Is it really true that African history began with the slave trade and colonial occupation, and that there was nothing worth writing about? No, no", thus reasoned the revisionist African historian.

In the mid-1950s, a Ghanaian named Dr de Graft Johnstone published a book titled *African Glory* in which he wrote in depth about the great African kingdoms of the past. Students of my generation had been taught that the *zimbabwe* – stone houses – in the country then called Southern Rhodesia had been built by an Asian race, or possibly Phoenicians. The natives living nearby, the Shona, were said to be too primitive and unintelligent to have built such castles.

Johnstone quoted 16th century Portuguese texts which stated that travellers had seen the people of Monomutapa, whom we now know as the Shona, building stone houses called *symbae*. In other words, the *zimbabwe* had been built by ancestors of the people living nearby.

African Glory was followed by *Old Africa Rediscovered*. This was the work of Basil Davidson, a Briton, whose lecture I attended in London in the 1960s. Davidson dug even deeper into the African past and made a startling revelation that before the advent of Egyptian civilisation, Egypt had been occupied by black people. He based his thesis on the findings of archaeologists and anthropologists who had come across negro skeletons there in Egypt. He cautiously stated that Egyptian civilisation might have been started by a negro race. But he did not supply adequate sources of information to convince the doubting Thomases.

It was left to a Senegalese, Professor Cheikh Anta Diop, to give what appears to those with open minds to be indisputable evidence of negro presence in pre-dynastic and even Pharaonic Egypt. Diop used four sources for his stance.

First is an evaluation of melanin levels. Melanin is a dark-brown to black pigment occurring in the hair, skin and iris of the eye. Secondly, he cites Greek historian, Herodotus, and Latin historian, Marcellinus, who described Egyptians as both brown and black. Thirdly, Diop compares the language of Pharaonic Egypt with West African languages. And, fourthly, Diop identifies the physical features of some of the Pharaohs as negroid rather than Semitic.

He first outlined his discoveries in his book *African Origin of Civilisation* and then elaborated on them in a chapter of a UNESCO book titled *General History of Africa*, subtitled *Ancient Civilisations of Africa*, edited by an Egyptian, G. Mokhtar.

Mokhtar says other scholars do not share Diop's views. Well, what do they say about the Sphinx which looks like a Bantu woman? And why do some Pharaohs look like Tutsis? Moreover, Pharaohs Thutmosis III, Sesostries and Narmer (or Menes) are depicted with broad noses and thick lips. Are these not black African physical features?

Index